LANGUAGE IN EDUCATION:
Theory and Practice
52

Alice C. Omaggio

Proficiency-Oriented Classroom Testing

Illustrated by Sonia Kundert

Published by
CAL Center for Applied Linguistics

Prepared by
ERIC® Clearinghouse on Languages and Linguistics

This publication was prepared with funding from the National Institute of Education, U.S. Department of Education under contract no. 400-82-0009. The opinions expressed in this report do not necessarily reflect the positions or policies of NIE or ED.

Language in Education: Theory and Practice

ISBN: 0-87281-324-X

July 1983

3520 Prospect Street NW
Washington DC 20007

Printed in the U.S.A.

LANGUAGE IN EDUCATION: THEORY AND PRACTICE

ERIC (Educational Resources Information Center) is a nationwide network of information centers, each responsible for a given educational level or field of study. ERIC is supported by the National Institute of Education of the U.S. Department of Education. The basic objective of ERIC is to make current developments in educational research, instruction, and personnel preparation more readily accessible to educators and members of related professions.

ERIC/CLL. The ERIC Clearinghouse on Languages and Linguistics (ERIC/CLL), one of the specialized clearinghouses in the ERIC system, is operated by the Center for Applied Linguistics. ERIC/CLL is specifically responsible for the collection and dissemination of information in the general area of research and application in languages, linguistics, and language teaching and learning.

LANGUAGE IN EDUCATION: THEORY AND PRACTICE. In addition to processing information, ERIC/CLL is also involved in information synthesis and analysis. The Clearinghouse commissions recognized authorities in languages and linguistics to write analyses of the current issues in their areas of specialty. The resultant documents, intended for use by educators and researchers, are published under the title Language in Education: Theory and Practice. The series includes practical guides for classroom teachers, extensive state-of-the-art papers, and selected bibliographies.

The material in this publication was prepared pursuant to a contract with the National Institute of Education, U.S. Department of Education. Contractors undertaking such projects under government sponsorship are encouraged to express freely their judgment in professional and technical matters. Prior to publication, the manuscript was submitted to the American Council on the Teaching of Foreign Languages for critical review and determination of professional competence. This publication has met such standards. Points of view or opinions, however, do not necessarily represent the official view or opinions of either ACTFL or NIE. This publication is not printed at the expense of the federal government.

This publication may be purchased directly from the Center for Applied Linguistics. It also will be announced in the ERIC monthly abstract journal Resources in Education (RIE) and will be available from the ERIC Document Reproduction Service, Computer Microfilm International Corp., P.O. Box 190, Arlington, VA 22210. See RIE for ordering information and ED number.

For further information on the ERIC system, ERIC/CLL, and Center/Clearinghouse publications, write to ERIC Clearinghouse on Languages and Linguistics, Center for Applied Linguistics, 3520 Prospect Street, N.W., Washington, D.C. 20007.

Sophia Behrens, editor

CONTENTS

INTRODUCTION

For many years, the major issues facing the foreign language teaching profession have been debated and discussed in terms of dichotomies. "We talk of methods as either inductive or deductive; of syllabuses as either structurally or situationally ordered; of learners as either instrumentally or integratively motivated" (Gaies 1980, p. 2). Likewise, language practice has been characterized as manipulative or communicative; language tests as discrete-point or integrative; learning environments as natural or contrived; language competence as learned or acquired. Although most educators realize that such terms represent opposite ends of a continuum, and that in reality, methods, syllabuses, learners, tests, and learning environments fall somewhere in between, the rhetoric of the language-teaching profession in the recent past has been, for the most part, focused on the contrasts and not on the commonalities in our thinking.

In the 1980s, however, a new unifying trend is emerging within the profession, indicating that foreign language educators might be ready at last for a consensus. There is no doubt that professional unity on a national scale has been prompted by the President's Commission on Foreign Language and International Studies. The National Conference on Professional Priorities, held in 1980 in Boston in conjunction with the ACTFL annual meeting, is one example of a direct effort to promote unification of purpose and action among language teachers in this country. Some of the recommendations emerging from that conference (Proceedings 1981) have begun to take root in various ways. The most important outcome has undoubtedly been the creation of the ACTFL/ETS "Stepladder Project,"[1] which is engaged in developing standard and universally acceptable language proficiency guidelines for listening, speaking, reading, writing, and culture across languages. These guidelines can be used to characterize any given language user's proficiency at any stage of development. (Sample provisionary guidelines for speaking are provided in Appendix B.)

There is little doubt that such a common standard of measurement is needed:[2] not only will it lead to better articulation between stages of language study in academic settings, but it will also enable teachers, students, and "consumers" to measure more accurately the <u>real</u> outcomes of instruction, thereby satisfying the needs of government, business, and industry to place language students appropriately in positions where foreign language skills are necessary. At the classroom level, such proficiency guidelines can serve to shape the future curriculum, when materials, activities, and achievement tests begin to reflect proficiency goals more directly (see Omaggio 1983). By arriving at a consensus about what language proficiency means, teachers will be able to measure outcomes against a common yardstick, and the profession will have come a long way toward establishing the unity that is absolutely vital to its own survival on the American scene.

What It Is to "Know" a Language

To arrive at a consensus about language proficiency, we as a profession must share a common understanding of what it is to know a language. What do students have to know, in terms of grammar, vocabulary, sound discrimination and production, sociolinguistic appropriateness, kinesics, cultural understanding, and the like in order to know a language well enough to use it for some real-world purpose? What should language learners be able to do at any given stage of proficiency, be it "novice," "intermediate," "advanced," "superior," or "near-native" in order to function in the language in some defined situation or capacity?[3]

The answers to such questions, though still the subject of some debate, seem to be coalescing in the recent literature on language competence. It is clear that definitions of language proficiency ought to include some reference to grammatical, sociolinguistic, strategic, and discourse competence, as defined by Canale and Swain (1981) and summarized in Appendix A of the Ontario Assessment Instrument Pool (1980). The essential characteristics of these facets of proficiency are summarized below:

Grammatical competence. Includes knowledge of lexical items and of rules of pronunciation/spelling, word formation, and sentence formation. Implies mastery of the features and rules of the language code itself. "Such competence is an important concern for any communicative approach whose goals include providing learners with the knowledge of how to understand and express accurately the literal meaning of utterances" (p. xxviii).

Sociolinguistic competence. Addresses the extent to which grammatical forms can be used or understood appropriately to communicate in various sociolinguistic contexts. Another concern is the degree of politeness conveyed.

Discourse competence. Involves mastery of combining sentences and ideas to achieve unified spoken or written text through cohesion in form and coherence in thought. "Cohesion deals with how utterances are linked structurally in a text and how the literal meaning of a text is interpreted....Coherence concerns the relationships among the different ideas in a text..." (p. xxix).

Strategic competence. Involves knowledge of verbal and nonverbal communication strategies that can be used to compensate for breakdowns in communication due to interference, distraction, or insufficient knowledge (pp. xxviii-xxx).

Note how the importance of grammatical accuracy, minimized somewhat in the 1970s with the rhetoric surrounding the term "communicative competence," has re-emerged in the newest definitions of this term as cited above. Higgs and Clifford (1982) argue that the grammaticality of utterances is a crucial factor in determining levels of language proficiency. They claim that definitions in the early and mid-1970s of "communicative competence," in which conveyance of one's essential meaning was considered to be of primary importance and accuracy of form was clearly secondary, "were based on faulty assumptions. A major problem with the popular definitions of "communicative competence" was that there was no analysis of the complexity of linguistic functions needed by communicators in a variety of real-world contexts beyond very elementary survival situations:

> Instead, the apparent assumption [was] that the same communication skills that allow one to obtain food in a restaurant would also serve to negotiate a business contract or an international treaty. Furthermore, little consideration [was] given to the accuracy of the message conveyed in terms of the hypothetical listener. Clearly, it is easier to order a meal than it is to convince a businessman through logical argumentation that his financial interests are best served by the firm or government one is representing (p. 59).

The question that must be asked, then, when determining the communicative competence of second language users is not "Were the students able to communicate?" but rather "What were they able to communicate, and how well?" The what refers to (1) the topic or context (message content) and (2) the language function to be performed in that context. The how well relates to the linguistic accuracy and cultural authenticity of the language produced. Function, content, and accuracy must serve as the three coexisting and interrelated hierarchies of judgmental criteria applied when describing all levels of language proficiency. These three interrelated criteria form the core of the newly revised (1982) Interagency Language Roundtable (ILR) definitions of proficiency described earlier and of the ACTFL/ETS Rating Scales. (See sample guidelines in Appendix B.) Without considering all three criteria, "...no judgment of general language proficiency or 'communicative competence' can be made" (Higgs and Clifford, p. 60).

Encouraging Accuracy in Early Language Learning

Recent research using performance profiles of second language learners at the CIA Language School has revealed another very interesting and significant phenomenon that has far-reaching implications for curriculum, methodology, and testing. It seems that attention to accuracy is fundamental in early language-learning situations if one is to attain more than a minimal competence in the second language. Recent analyses of students who have not been able to meet performance standards at ILR Level 3 or better have led to the discovery of the phenomenon referred to as the "terminal 2."

> The rating is associated with students who enter training with a level 2 proficiency but who peak out at level 2+. They do not progress to level 3, and thus never attain the linguistic skills needed to reach minimum job proficiency standards (Higgs and Clifford, p. 65).

In other words, the fossilized lexical and grammatical structures that these students have acquired are generally _not_ remediable. There is also a terminal profile that has been identified at the 1+ level, usually the product of "street learning." The authors argue that it is the existence of these cases of fossilized language behavior that should make us reconsider the push of the 1970s toward "communication" without adequate concern for linguistic accuracy.

> The terminal cases whose foreign language background had included only an academic environment all came from language programs that either were taught by instructors who themselves had not attained grammatical mastery of the target language--and hence were not able to guide their students into correct usage--or by instructors who had chosen not to correct their students' mistakes for philosophical, methodological, or personal reasons (Higgs and Clifford, p. 68).

The implications for curriculum, methodology, and testing are clear: a concern for accuracy seems to be vital to the eventual "linguistic health" of learners who wish to progress beyond the survival level in their skill development.

A decision to strive for linguistic accuracy from the beginning of language instruction does _not_ imply a de-emphasis of communicative language use in the classroom.

> No reasoned interpretation of the data suggests a return to grammar-translation or classical mim-mem audiolingual methodologies. What is implied is the systematic recognition of the _ultimate_ role that linguistic accuracy plays in the achievement of true communicative competence, in which it truly does matter _how_ the message is transmitted (Higgs and Clifford, p. 77).

Teaching for accuracy, then, should not negate the value of communicative language use as a goal of instruction, nor of approaches to language learning that encourage functional language use in context. Rather than continuing to think in terms of dichotomies, contrasting "linguistic competence" with "communicative competence," we should be thinking instead of achieving a coalescence of all relevant performance factors when we speak of "communication" as an instructional goal.

The implications of the Higgs and Clifford research as well as of the theoretical work of Canale and Swain (1981) are clear for all types of language testing. There is no doubt that we are making great strides as a profession in developing better general or "absolute"[4] proficiency tests that will measure language proficiency through a merger of the criteria of function, content, and accuracy. We cannot generally claim the same progress, however, in classroom achievement testing. In fact, few classroom achievement tests reflect the thinking of the 1970s, let alone the 1980s. They tend to be largely discrete-point in nature, reflecting behavioristic language-learning theories popular two decades ago, and testing linguistic accuracy almost always out of context. It is this incongruence between our common proficiency goal statements as a profession and the course-specific achievement tests by which we typically measure those goals at the classroom level that will be addressed in this publication.

Testing Achievement in the Classroom: A Need for Reappraisal

Approaches to language teaching have undergone some extraordinary changes in the past twenty years, yet traditional methods of evaluating progress have been conserved in most foreign language classrooms. This situation has resulted in an ever-widening gap between the description of course goals--often in terms of proficiency statements--and their measurement. Such a gap can erode or even destroy the effect that a particular curricular revision was meant to produce, no matter how innovative or creative the new materials or methods might be. This is true because the nature of evaluation, "...that is, the content of the tests and the method by which grades are assigned, reflects more accurately than any lengthy statement of aims and purposes the real objectives of instruction" (Valette 1978, p. 90). As Bartz (1976) stated in an article on testing communication skills:

> If the message to the students in today's classroom is that they should be able to communicate in the foreign language, tests which measure their ability to communicate must be administered. A close look at testing in today's foreign language classroom, however, reveals quite clearly that such a message is not being conveyed.

> Instead, the message is that the <u>real objective</u> of foreign language instruction is the development of the ability to carry out abundant grammatical exercises (pp. 52-53).

Figure 1, an excerpt from a typical achievement test in first-year college French, shows quite clearly how many current classroom tests convey that message.

Of the three criteria for proficiency testing mentioned earlier--function, content, and accuracy--only the third is represented to any extent on this classroom achievement test. Language is not being tested as it functions naturally in a context; rather, it is being tested in a "piecemeal" fashion, with no logical continuation between items in terms of their content. It is true that in most sections of the test a sentence-length "context" has been provided. Yet it is usually not necessary to read the whole sentence in order to fill in the correct answer. Hosenfeld's research (1976) has shown that many students successfully "short-circuit" test items of this type, a fact that contributes further to the impression that many students have: success on language tests involves learning grammatical "tricks" rather than processing language meaningfully in a larger context.

In sections I through V of this book, alternative formats for classroom achievement testing will be presented and discussed. These formats are suggested as a possible starting point for revising classroom tests so that they reflect language proficiency goals more directly; that is, classroom achievement tests, like general proficiency tests, should focus on context, function, and accuracy by presenting language in "naturalistic" or "authentic" contexts. Only then will success on course-specific achievement tests relate in any direct way to improvement in "absolute" proficiency, as measured on such general proficiency tests as the ILR interview.

The item formats suggested here, then, are "proficiency-oriented," yet they still retain some of the characteristics of achievement tests, since test items are structured to provide specific feedback on the mastery of course-specific material. These same formats can be adapted and used for classroom instructional activities as well. In fact, since a test is fundamentally a task to be observed and evaluated, it seems logical, and indeed advisable, that we use the same types of tasks in language practice activities as we use in testing.

The Case for "Hybrid" Classroom Tests

In order to revise our present classroom tests, it is not enough to simply "tack on" a few global or communicative items to an existing "traditional" test instrument such as the one in Figure 1, or to administer periodically a few "communication"

Fig. 1. "Typical" grammar test items.

I. Fill in the blanks with the preposition à or de where necessary. (10 points)

A. Je ne regrette pas _____ être étudiant à cette université.
B. Il n'a pas commencé _____ apprendre un métier.
C. Mon prof m'a conseillé _____ venir en classe tous les jours.
D. Je déteste _____ l'été parce qu'il fait trop chaud....

II. Complete the translations. (6 points)

A. __________, on exprime ses opinions. *By voting, one expresses one's opinion.*
B. Hier, ils ont acheté __________. *Yesterday, they bought an interesting book.*
C. Mon père nous a raconté __________. *My father told us a shocking story.*
D. __________ est un droit. *Voting is a right.*

III. Fill in the blanks with the correct form of the subjunctive of the verb indicated. (25 points)

A. Il faut qu'ils __________ me voir.
(venir)
B. Il est possible que je __________ à la maison ce soir.
(être)
C. *Il est possible que nous __________ de l'argent....*
(avoir)

IV. Substitutions. Replace the underlined words with the words in parentheses and make all necessary changes. (20 points)

A. D'habitude, je me levais à 7 heures. (hier)
B. Vous recevez de jolis cadeaux. (tu)....

(I. A. I do not regret _____ being a student at this university.
B. He has not begun _____ learn a trade.
C. My professor advised me _____ come to class every day.
D. I hate _____ summer because it's too hot.

III. A. It's necessary that they __________ see me. (to come)
B. It is possible that I __________ at home this evening. (to be)
C. It is possible that we __________ some money. (to have)

IV. A. Usually, I got up at 7:00. (yesterday)
B. You receive pretty gifts. (you, familiar form))

tests and average them somehow into a final grade. Such an approach would serve to reconfirm the impression students may already have that learning the phonology, grammar, and vocabulary of the foreign language is one thing, and using the language in some genuine fashion is another. Instead, it seems that we need to develop a kind of "hybrid" testing program, devising achievement tests in which naturalistic, communicative language is used as much as possible. Traditional discrete-point item formats built around random lists of disconnected sentences have no place on such an exam. All items should be embedded in naturalistic discourse-length contexts rather than in single-phrase or sentence-length frames.

Wesche (1981) supports this point of view in her discussion of communicative testing, pointing out the importance of testing language use beyond the sentence level:

> Language testing which does not take into account propositional and illocutionary development beyond the sentence level, as well as the interaction between language behavior and real-world phenomenon, is at best getting at only a part of communicative competence. Small wonder that we often find that a student's success at second-language classroom exercises and tests appears to bear little relationship to his or her ability to use the language effectively in a real-world situation (pp. 552-53).

She goes on to argue that natural language always occurs in both a discourse context and an extralinguistic context, and that therefore, "the language and the tasks that we use in our tests must have the characteristics of real language in use" (p. 553). Furthermore, "research suggests that second languages are best acquired as well as tested through their naturalistic use in context" (p. 554). Another consideration is the high motivational value of teaching and testing language skills in realistic contexts. Students feel that language learning is more relevant when the tasks they are asked to do resemble authentic language use situations. Shohamy (1982) found that students had a favorable attitude toward oral interviews, for example, for this reason.

If we accept the premise that the language presented on the test instrument should be contextualized and integrative in nature, it is clear that we must abandon the single-sentence formats typically used in the past in achievement testing. Yet because we are giving <u>achievement</u> tests throughout the course of instruction more often than we administer <u>proficiency</u> tests, we still need to be able to analyze our students' performance in terms of specific course objectives: that is, the specific grammar and vocabulary items to be mastered in a given unit of study need to be <u>elicited</u> directly on the test instrument in order to provide information on mastery of the material and specific diagnostic feedback. The "trick," then, that must be mastered in designing achievement tests is to create an examination that will elicit specified features of the target language within naturalistic discourse.

The "hybrid" tests described in the following pages are an attempt to do this by "artfully combining grammar and context, structure and situation" (Slager 1978). On such tests, some items might be open-ended, while others require more specific, convergent answers. Sections of the test that focus on discrete points of grammar or vocabulary, blended in a naturalistic context, enable teachers to test for mastery of specific features of the language and to provide more specific feedback on recently learned material than is often possible on more global proficiency tests.

While some open-ended or global item types might be included in each unit test or quiz, separate, more extensive oral or written general achievement tests might also be scheduled as part of the overall testing program, enabling the teacher to determine how well students have synthesized all the information learned thus far in a given course of study. Of course, at any time an instructor may also wish to conduct an oral interview or other general proficiency test to determine the students' overall level of proficiency on a scale such as the one being developed by ACTFL and ETS.

Characterizing Test Items and Item Types

In order to compare traditional testing methods with the methods to be proposed in the following sections, it would be useful to classify test item types in some way. Figure 2 presents a schema by which test items can be located on a set of two intersecting axes.

The vertical axis represents a continuum relating to the "naturalness" of the language on the test. Items at the top portion of the continuum would be rather unnatural, in terms of their relationship to genuine language in use, whereas items at the bottom of the continuum would be taken directly from natural discourse. For example, the series of single-sentence frames on the typical French test in Figure 1 would fall along the top portion of the continuum, since there is no logical continuation between sentences, and the language is rather stilted. If, on the other hand, the test items were created from genuine discourse, and each sentence followed the one before it logically, the test would fall within the bottom portion of the continuum, toward "natural language." The hybrid test consists of items drawn mainly from this latter end of the continuum: the language of the test approaches natural discourse, either by providing a situationalized context for the test items or by embedding them in a context created for the test or adapted from genuine texts.

Fig. 2. Locating test items.

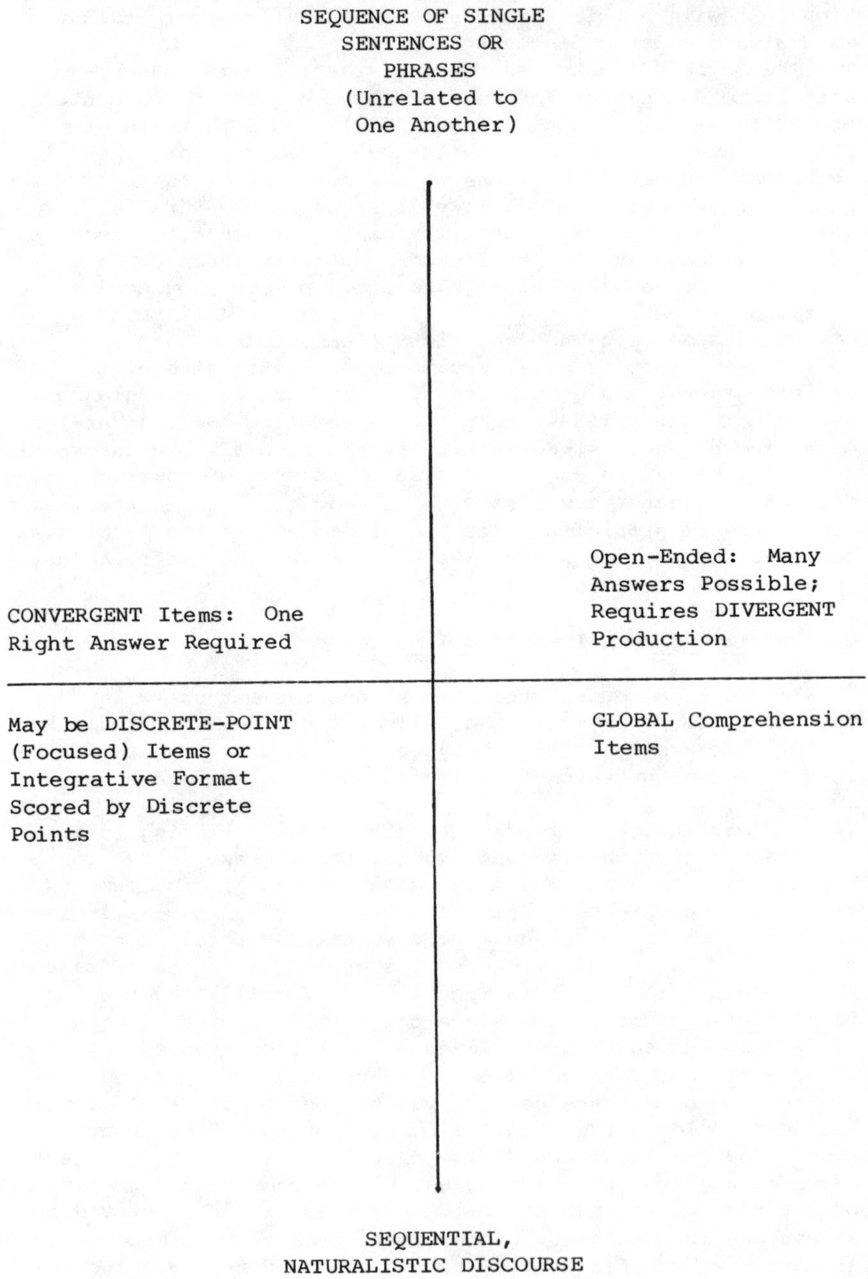

SEQUENCE OF SINGLE SENTENCES OR PHRASES (Unrelated to One Another)

Open-Ended: Many Answers Possible; Requires DIVERGENT Production

CONVERGENT Items: One Right Answer Required

May be DISCRETE-POINT (Focused) Items or Integrative Format Scored by Discrete Points

GLOBAL Comprehension Items

SEQUENTIAL, NATURALISTIC DISCOURSE

In creating contexts for test items, Slager (1978) suggests the following principles:

- The situation depicted should be relevant and immediately useful to language learners.
- The content should reflect the level of sophistication of the students and their knowledge of the world.
- The language should be natural at all times, respecting the "conditions of elicitation" of certain types of structures in natural language use.
- Answers required of students should have "truth value."
- Characters used in items should be "realistic" in that they have personality and relate to the learner's experience in some way.
- Items should respect sociolinguistic norms.
- The language sample should be short enough so that students have little difficulty remembering it, but long enough to provide the necessary context.[5]

The horizontal axis in Figure 2 represents the specificity of test items, ranging from those on the left requiring the most "convergent" or discrete-point answers, to those on the right requiring more global comprehension and/or "divergent" production. In order to blend linguistic and communicative testing procedures, achievement tests should include items from various points along this continuum. If one again considers the sample test items in the traditional grammar test in Figure 1, it is clear that they would all fall along the extreme left-hand portion of the horizontal axis. Consequently, this type of test would not reflect proficiency to any extent. Students are not required to synthesize the bits and pieces of language they have been learning for some real-world purpose. In contrast to this, the hybrid test, which is "proficiency oriented," requires both meaningful processing and some type of synthesis of linguistic elements for virtually every item on the test. Communicative language use underlies the entire testing program, and each individual test, by its very nature, illustrates to students that mastery of discrete points of grammar and lexicon has a "real-world" communicative function.

In the next pages, some initial ideas for contextualizing test items in all four skill areas will be presented, and various levels of grammatical and lexical specificity will be illustrated. Mixed-skills items will also be discussed. Ideas for oral proficiency testing, including interviews based on the

ACTFL/ETS Rating Scales (see Appendix B) will be presented in Section IV. Following the description of item types, concrete suggestions for creating tests of this type will be offered. Several examples of hour-long unit exams for college French and Spanish courses will be presented in Appendix A to illustrate how the combination of various types of items can be achieved.

Most testing formats will be appropriate for beginning and intermediate levels of foreign language instruction in four-skill courses, but some ideas might also be adaptable to other types of courses as curricular options continue to expand in the future.

I. LISTENING COMPREHENSION FORMATS

Tests of listening skills are perhaps among the easiest to contextualize; considerable progress has been made in the past few years in the development of ideas for testing "pure" listening comprehension by using simulated communicative settings. Bartz (1976), Schulz and Bartz (1975), Linder (1977), and Valette (1977) present a variety of suggestions for listening test formats, with item types ranging from those requiring the student to make fairly discrete decisions to those in which global comprehension is measured. Other sources for listening comprehension formats with a communicative focus can be found in Howard (1980), Mauriac (1980), and in the Ontario Assessment Instrument Pool (1980). Examples of these ideas will be included in this section.

The following are some basic formats for contextualized listening tests, synthesized and adapted from the literature on foreign language testing. Item types are listed in the order of their specificity in terms of task demands, with those requiring more discrete answers listed first. Note that items fall within the lower portion of the vertical continuum (See Figure 2), since they approximate natural, connected discourse. All items are based on a passage in the target language, read either once or twice, depending on the level of difficulty of the speech sample and on the short-term memory load associated with the task.

When discussing classroom test formats, it is important to bear in mind that achievement testing is a formative evaluation process: in testing situations as well as in instruction, the goal should be to lead the learners toward eventual comprehension of genuine language used in a communicative context. This goal might best be achieved through successive approximations of authentic language in use. That is, for beginning students, listening passages should consist of short, simplified approximations of natural language rather than authentic texts, since it is unrealistic to expect the novice to comprehend unedited speech delivered at native speed, especially under the pressures of a testing situation. (Test passages, though contextualized, might seem stilted and somewhat artificial at this stage of instruction.)

In addition, it is advisable to provide a second reading of the passage for beginning students, whose short-term memory is effectively shortened due to unfamiliarity with the new code. When students' skills have progressed beyond the "novice" level, listening tasks may be structured to approximate more closely authentic discourse, and repetition of listening passages may be eliminated. These test items illustrate the variety of language samples one might choose for listening comprehension tasks, depending on the level of proficiency expected of learners at a given stage of instruction.

A. Grammatical or Lexical Cues

A passage is read and the student is required to listen for specific lexical or grammatical features embedded in the selection. Some sample grammatical features might include listening for cues to tense, gender, number, and the like. In the example given in French below, students listen for cues to tense in a short passage.

Sample 1.

> Imagine you are sitting in a cafe in Paris and are overhearing snatches of conversation. Can you tell whether the speakers are talking about present or past events? Listen carefully for the verbs in each conversation. If you hear a verb in the past, mark column A. If you hear a verb in the present, mark column B. There are x verbs in each conversation.

Short conversational exchanges are then read or played on tape. In each conversation, a given number of verbs are embedded, either in the present or in the past. The conversation is played or read once. Then each sentence is read individually and students mark the appropriate column for each verb they hear.[6]

Although the task described above is set up so that students listen for discrete morphological cues to tense, the fact that the listening passage is contextualized will mean that the results will be somewhat less diagnostic than those obtained with the isolated sentence-length format. This is due to the fact that natural language often provides extraneous cues to tense, such as time words or overall situational cues not available in a single sentence. However, the contextualized format has the advantage of encouraging students to derive meaning from various types of cues, both contextual and structural.

B. Recording Semantic Details

A passage is read and the student takes notes on specific semantic information in the native language, follows a map or diagram, responds to preposed questions in the native language, or fills in an incomplete chart, schedule, table, or other type of form provided on the test paper.

Listening items of this type still require students to listen for specific details, but the details recorded are semantic, rather than syntactic, in nature. The following example in French asks students to listen for specific information from the listening passage (disregarding other irrelevant details) and take notes on the information needed in English on the form provided.

Sample 1.

(The passage describes an apartment for rent, indicating location, price, number and size of rooms, utilities, etc.)

a) Location: ______________________________

b) Price: ______________________________

c) Number and type of rooms: _______________

____

d) Furnishings:
(Check one) _ Furnished _ Unfurnished

e) Utilities:
(Check one) _ Not included _ Included in rent

f) Type of utilities: (Check all that apply)
_ Gas _ Electricity _ Telephone

g) Nearest Metro stop: ____________________

h) Phone number of landlord: _______________

Sample 2.

You will hear a passage read twice. Here is the menu for Chez Madeleine; circle what Annick has for dinner and answer the questions in English.

Chez Madeleine

Hors-d'oeuvres

Oeufs à la mayonnaise
Pâté de campagne
Sardines à l'huile

Entrées

Soupe de poisson
Escargots
Salade de tomates

Plats principaux

Porc à la française
Escalope de veau
à la crème
Bifteck au poivre
Rôti de boeuf

Légumes

Petits pois
Haricots verts
Asperges

Fromages

Camembert
Brie

Desserts

Tarte aux pommes
Glace au chocolat
Tarte aux fraises
Mousse au chocolat

Boissons

Eau minérale
Café
Vin rouge
Vin rosé
Vin blanc

(Hors-d'oeuvres

Eggs in mayonnaise
Country-style pâté
Sardines in oil

Entrees

Fish soup
Snails
Tomato salad

Main Courses

French-style pork
Veal cutlet in cream sauce
Pepper steak
Roast beef

Vegetables

Peas
Green beans
Asparagus

Cheeses

Camembert
Brie

Desserts

Apple tart
Chocolate ice cream
Strawberry tart
Chocolate mousse)

Beverages

Mineral water
Coffee
Red wine
Rosé wine
White wine

a) At what time are Annick and Paul eating at the restaurant?
b) How much does Annick's meal cost?
c) How much does Paul's meal cost?
d) What happens at the end of the passage? What would you do in this situation?

Read the following listening comprehension passage twice at a normal rate, pausing between readings to allow students to answer the questions.

"C'est l'anniversaire d'Annick. Elle va dîner avec son ami Paul au restaurant "Chez Madeleine" à 7h30 du soir. Annick aime beaucoup ce restaurant et elle a l'intention de beaucoup manger.

D'abord elle prend du pâté de campagne comme hors-d'oeuvre et de la soupe de poisson comme entrée. Puis elle commande du rôti de boeuf comme plat principal et des haricots verts comme légume. Il y a de la salade verte et du camembert aussi. Bien sûr, elle commande du dessert; c'est de la tarte aux fraises. Annick et Paul boivent de l'eau minérale et du vin rouge.

Le repas d'Annick coûte 73 francs. Le repas de Paul coûte cher aussi: son repas coûte 85 francs. Paul veut payer l'addition mais il n'a pas assez d'argent. Qu'est-ce qu'il peut faire?"

(It's Annick's birthday. She is going to have dinner with her friend Paul at Chez Madeleine [a restaurant] at 7:30 p.m. Annick likes this restaurant and she intends to eat a lot. First she has some pâté as an hors-d'oeuvre and fish soup as an entrée. Then she orders some roast beef as a main course and green beans for the vegetable. There's green salad and some camembert cheese also. Of course, she orders dessert: she chooses strawberry tart. Annick and Paul drink some mineral water and red wine. Annick's meal costs 73 francs. Paul's meal is expensive too: his costs 85 francs. Paul wants to pay the check but he doesn't have enough money. What can he do?)[7]

An example of a listening item in German in which students complete a picture is given below.

Sample 3.

You will hear a listening passage about Oliver's room. As you listen to the passage, draw and label the items Oliver rearranges in his bedroom according to the information you hear. You will hear the passage twice. Label the items in English or German, according to your preference.

"Oliver will sein Zimmer neudekorieren und aufräumen. Erst stellt er den Nachttisch neben das Bett; dann stellt er den Tisch vor das Fenster, zwischen das Bett und das Sofa. Er setzt drei Stühle an der Tisch. Links, neben die Tür, stellt er ein Bücherregal. Seine zwei Bilder hängt er an die Wand übers Bett. Die Kissen kommen auf das Sofa und die Stehlampe links, in die Ecke, neben das Sofa."

(Oliver wants to redecorate and tidy up his room. First he puts the night stand next to the bed; then he puts the table in front of the window, in between the bed and the sofa. He places three chairs at the table. On the left, next to the door, he sets a bookshelf. He hangs his two posters on the wall over the bed. The cushions go on the sofa and the floor lamp to the left, in the corner, next to the sofa.)

Student copy: Complete the picture, according to the information you hear in the passage.[8]

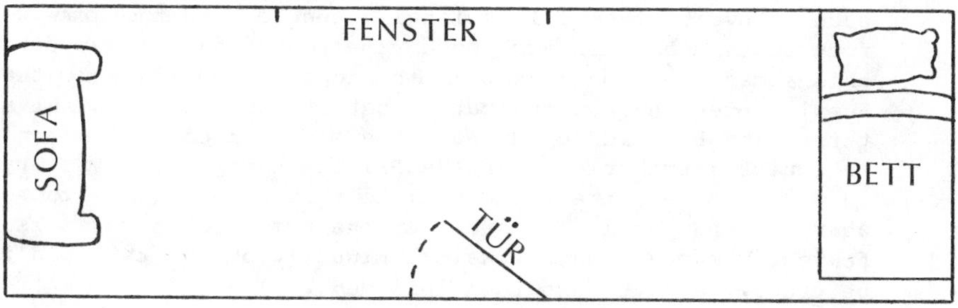

FENSTER
SOFA
BETT
TÜR

The item in Spanish below could best be reserved for somewhat more advanced students, since some inferencing is required. The passage should be read with pauses, as indicated by the double slash marks, to assure that students' memory is not overloaded and to allow them time to formulate an answer. The answer to question (6) can be written in English (and scored for its value as a global "recap" of the passage by virtue of whether it logically concludes the story), or in Spanish, making it a creative writing item. The drawback of the latter course, however, is that the writing item is totally dependent on the listening comprehension skills of the student, and the student might be doubly penalized for a listening error. This option may be better if the item is used for reading comprehension with a creative writing follow-up.

Sample 4.

"Interrumpimos el programa que están mirando ahora para informarles de estos acontecimientos urgentes y de interés mundial. //Nos hemos enterado, hace unos ratos por la UPI, que una brigada inglesa acaba de atacar la puerta de Buenos Aires, capturando toda la capital en un estado de sorpresa total. //Se ha transmitido que no se sospechaba tal novedad puesto que toda la atención nacional y el ejército se enfocaban en esas islas cuyo nombre ahora no se recuerda. //En este momento, no se sabe si el reportaje es válido, pero en la prensa rusa se ha communicado que en la madre patria, un grupo de argentinos terroristas han secuestrado a la primera ministra en un acto de retribución. //Si los ingleses logran un triunfo en Buenos Aires, el mundo estará esperando nerviosamente para ver lo que pasará en Inglaterra. Es que ahora se teme lo peor. //Un momento...un momento...oh no, que no puede ser...acabamos de informarnos que...."

(We interrupt the program you are watching now to bring you news of these urgent happenings of world interest. We have just been informed, via UPI, that British ships have just attacked the port of Buenos Aires, taking the capital totally by surprise. It is reported that no one suspected such an event since all national attention and the army were focused on those islands whose name nobody can remember. At this moment, we don't know if the report is valid, but the Russian press has communicated that a group of Argentinian terrorists has kidnapped the Prime Minister of England in an act of retribution. If the British carry off a victory in Buenos Aires, the world will be waiting nervously to see what will happen in England. At the moment, the worst is feared. Just a minute...wait a minute...oh no, this can't be true...we have just been informed....)

a) Who is talking? To whom?
b) What has just happened (first piece of information)?
c) Why was this such a surprise?
d) What piece of information has just appeared in print?
e) Why is the world on tenterhooks?
f) What is the outcome? (Provide, in English, your own ending to the story.)[9]

C. Comprehension Questions

A passage is read and the student answers a set of true/false, multiple-choice, or completion questions (in English) on the passage content or on inferences one might make from the passage content. Many teachers have used this format for listening and reading tests, but often mix skills by requiring students to answer in the target language. There is nothing wrong with having students answer this way, but teachers must keep in mind that they are testing reading, listening, and sometimes writing skills in an integrative fashion and thereby losing some diagnostic power. Mixed-skills test items will be discussed later.

An example of a listening passage in French with a set of true/false items in English is given in the following second-semester unit exam item.

Sample 1.

You will hear a passage read twice by your instructor. Listen carefully; then answer the true/false questions below, basing your answers on the passage content.

a) T F The passage says that by 8 o'clock in the morning, most people are already at work.
b) T F According to the passage, more and more people have recently been taking their cars to get to work.
c) T F The bicycle is generally used for sports and leisure activities on week-ends.
d) T F The bicycle industry is a great success in France.
e) T F Even some businessmen would like to exchange their Rolls Royces for a bicycle.

Read the passage at normal conversational speed. Give the students a chance to answer the questions, and then read the passage through once more.

"Huit heures du matin: les rues sont pleines de monde; les jeunes vont à l'école ou à l'université; les adultes vont à leur travail. Tout le monde est pressé. Mais comment tous ces gens vont-ils à leur travail respectif? En autobus? Oui, souvent. A pied? Quelquefois, si la distance n'est pas trop grande. En voiture? Oui, mais de moins en moins. Maintenant, c'est la bicyclette qui est à la mode.

Partout, la popularité de la bicyclette est énorme. Le vélo n'est pas simplement un amusement pour les enfants ou pour les sportifs, c'est un véritable moyen de transport. En Amérique les cyclistes sont plus de 100 millions. En France, un Français sur trois possède une bicyclette. L'exportation des bicyclettes est maintenant un des grands succès de l'industrie française. Même certains hommes d'affaires préfèrent une bicyclette à leur Rolls Royce."

Key: (a) F (b) F (c) F (d) T (e) T

(Eight o'clock in the morning: the streets are full of people; young people are going to school or to the university; adults are going off to work. Everyone is in a hurry. But how do all these people get to their respective jobs? By bus? Often, yes. On foot? Sometimes, if the distance isn't too great. In a car? Yes, but less and less often. Now, it's the bicycle that's in style.

Everywhere, the bicycle is enormously popular. The bike is not just a toy for children or an amusement for those who enjoy sports, it's a real means of transportation. In the U.S. there are more than 100 million cyclists. In France, one in three Frenchmen has a bicycle. Bicycle exportation is currently one of the great successes of French industry. Even some businessmen prefer a bicycle to their Rolls Royce.)[10]

A more complicated, lengthy listening passage, used on a general achievement test in French at the fourth-semester level, is illustrated below. Students are directed to read through the English multiple-choice questions on their test papers first. Then the passage is read twice, once with slight pauses (indicated by // marks) so students can make their choices, and a second time with no pauses.

Sample 2.

You will hear a short segment of an interview with a professor at a French university about student-teacher relationships. Listen to the passage carefully. Then answer the multiple-choice questions below on the passage content. You will hear the passage twice.

a) The interviewer states that professors in France are accused of

1) being too strict with students.
2) being unavailable to students.
3) ignoring students' needs and opinions.

b) According to the professor being interviewed, students
1) take advantage of his office hours.
2) come to see him on Thursday afternoons.
3) rarely make or keep appointments with him.

c) The professor feels frustrated because
1) students complain about his unavailability, even though he keeps regular office hours.
2) students expect to get good grades without working.
3) no one understands that professors need time to do research and cannot always be available to students.

d) According to the professor being interviewed, instructors at Yale
1) are expected to cater to students' needs much more than professors in France do.
2) are generally paid very well, but do not have as many responsibilities as professors in France.
3) are treated much more like individuals than professors in France are.

e) If one were to compare the American and French systems, one would conclude that
1) American professors are to be praised for their concern for students.
2) French professors are too severe with students.
3) the two systems operate on different sociological principles.

"(Interviewer): On reproche souvent aux professeurs français de n'être pas assez disponibles avec leurs étudiants. Qu'en pensez-vous?// (Professeur): Je ne crois pas que cela soit tout à fait exact. Mes étudiants, par exemple, savent que je suis dans mon bureau tous les jeudi après-midi, au moins deux heures avant le cours. En général, il n'en vient jamais.//Alors, il est fort possible que les mêmes étudiants, si vous alliez les interroger, vous disent: 'Ah, Monsieur Arnaud, on ne peut jamais lui parler, il n'est jamais là!' (ce qui est faux). Alors, vous comprenez, c'est un peu agaçant de savoir que personne ne viendra vous voir et d'être critiqué en même temps pour son manque de disponibilité.//

C'est là qu'il y a une différence avec les Etats-Unis. J'ai eu souvent l'impression dans les universités où je suis allé, en particulier à Yale, que l'enseignant était souvent considéré comme un individu sur lequel on avait des droits parce qu'on avait payé en général très cher et parce qu'il était normal que cette personne reste à votre disposition. //Cette attitude représente donc sans doute un excès inverse si on la compare avec les pratiques françaises. Vous voyez, il ne suffit pas de marquer les différences, de louer les professeurs américains ou d'être sévère avec les universitaires français. Il faut bien comprendre que ces deux systèmes supposent une sociologie tout à fait différente."

(Interviewer: People often complain that French professors are not available enough to their students. What do you think about that?// Professor: I don't think that that's exactly true. My students, for example, know that I am in my office every Thursday afternoon, at least two hours before class. In general, they never come.//However, it's very possible that those same students, if you were to interview them, would say: 'Oh, Mr. Arnaud, you can never talk to him, he's never there' (which is not true). So, you see, it's a little irritating to know that nobody will come see you and to be criticized at the same time for your lack of availability.//

That's where there's a difference in the United States. I have often had the impression at the universities where I have gone, particularly at Yale, that the instructor was often considered as an individual over whom one had a certain control, because you had generally paid a lot for your education and because it was normal to expect that person to be at your disposal.//This attitude represents, undoubtedly, the opposite extreme if you compare it with French practices. You see, it's not enough to note the differences, to praise American professors or to be severely critical of French faculty. You have to understand that the two systems are based on entirely different sociological principles.)[11]

D. Native Language Summary

A passage is read and the student writes a summary of the message content in the native language. Items of this type allow students somewhat more freedom in answering, since they can select whatever information they wish to include in their résumés. Grading of these items should be done in an objective fashion, and there are some excellent ideas for scoring such listening tests in Linder (1977), Schulz and Bartz (1976), and Valette (1977). Briefly, points can be awarded for each piece of information remembered correctly, with points deducted for wrong information, and some type of objective formulae developed for rewarding specificity of detail.

An example in Spanish for a third-semester exam is given below:

Sample 1.

You will hear a paragraph read twice in Spanish. Record as much information as you can in ENGLISH. Complete sentences are not necessary. (Scored by tallying the number of legitimate facts and inferences listed by the top 10% of the papers and prorating on the basis of a total score of 12.)

"Una persona de mala educación robó el hogar de ancianos el otro día. Los ancianos lloraban y rezaban cuando el hombre pidió todo su dinero. Algunas viudas, que no gozaban de buena salud, casi murieron de la experiencia desagradable. Afortunadamente, un vecino extranjero llamó la policía. Cuando arrestaron al joven soltero, estaba muy avergonzado."

(A poorly educated person robbed a home for the aged the other day. The old people cried and prayed when the man took all of their money. Some widows, who were not in good health, almost died from the unpleasant experience. Fortunately, a foreign neighbor called the police. When they arrested the single young man, he was very ashamed.)12

E. Global Classification

A passage is read and the student writes or chooses from several options an appropriate title, creates or chooses from options the best "moral" of the story or summary of the main idea, or classifies the passage type in some other global way. Although the task demands of this type of listening item are clearly global in nature, the scoring procedures are often simpler and more objective than in item D. Students select the correct answer from options or write an answer in English that is judged as correct or incorrect on the basis of some clearly defined criterion.

Sample 1.

Listen to the following announcement to decide what the speaker is promoting. Then circle the letter of the correct answer. Look first at the possibilities on your page. The speaker is promoting:

a) a taxi service
b) a hotel
c) an airport
d) a restaurant

"Idéalement situé...Service de transport de l'aéroport international...Quarante-deux chambres luxueuses, climatisées...Elégant restaurant...De réputation internationale."

Ecoutez encore une fois. (Passage is repeated.) Encerclez la lettre de la réponse correcte sur votre page.

("Ideally located...transportation service to and from the international airport...forty-two luxurious air-conditioned rooms...elegant restaurant...international reputation.")[13]

Sample 2.

Listen to the following short conversation between Paul and Marie. Choose the sentence that best describes what you have heard and circle the letter of the correct answer. First look at the possible answers on your page:

a) Paul asks if Suzanne is sick.
b) Marie insists that Suzanne is not sick.
c) Marie will find out if Suzanne is sick.
d) Marie insists that Suzanne is sick.

Paul: Tu sais, ton amie Suzanne est absente encore une fois! Quelle fille! Si elle ne veut pas aller à l'école, elle dit qu'elle est malade.
Marie: Sa mère dit qu'elle a de la fièvre.
Paul: Je te dis qu'elle n'est pas malade!
Marie: Mais si! Je t'assure qu'elle est très malade!

Ecoutez encore une fois. (The passage is repeated.) Encerclez la lettre de la réponse correcte sur votre page.

(Paul: You know, your friend Suzanne is absent again! What a girl! If she doesn't want to go to school, she says she's sick.
Marie: Her mother says she has a fever.
Paul: I tell you she's not sick!
Marie: Oh yes she is! I assure you she's really sick!)[14]

F. Identifying Sociolinguistic Factors

A statement is read, and the student must indicate in English an understanding of the sociolinguistic context in which such a statement might be made. This type of listening item is suggested by Howard (1980).

Sample 1.

Consider the following. "Je vous en prie, Marie, fermez-moi cette porte tout de suite!" (Please, Marie, would you shut that door this minute!) Tell in English

a) where this statement may be heard (setting);
b) under what circumstances (nature of language event);
c) why the person is saying this (purpose);
d) what tone the person probably uses (mood);
e) who the speaker may be (status or role);
f) to whom the person is speaking (status);
g) how the speaker feels (attitude).[15]

Howard states that in this item, both grammatical and lexical correctness are tested in relationship to sociolinguistic considerations. The item actually invites the learner to infer the context of a single statement rather than to interpret the statement in the light of a context already provided on the test.

II. READING COMPREHENSION FORMATS

The item formats described for listening comprehension can be easily adapted for reading comprehension. Items can require students to show mastery of reading vocabulary or grammar--as in format (A) above; they may ask students to extract specific semantic information from a reading passage--formats (B) and (C); they may require synthesis of the information in some more global way--formats (D) and (E), or they may ask students to assign sociolinguistic meaning to an utterance or short conversation or passage--format (F).

A. Grammatical or Lexical Cues

An example of an item in which the focus is placed on specific grammatical features of the language (such as direct and indirect object pronouns) is given below. This sample item tests both grammatical competence and discourse competence within the context of a unified reading passage. Discourse competence is tested by asking the learner to understand object pronouns (the grammatical elements) as cohesive devices in discourse, choosing the referents to those pronouns correctly from extracts of a connected passage.

Sample 1.

Les phrases suivantes sont tirées d'un passage sur la publicité. Pouvez-vous identifier l'idée ou le nom associé au pronom souligné?

a) La publicité est l'ensemble des moyens employés pour faire connaître les produits commerciaux, pour les vanter.
   1) les moyens
   2) les produits commerciaux
   3) l'ensemble

b) L'homme normal a le goût de l'information. C'est pour lui une curiosité et un besoin.
   1) l'homme normal
   2) le goût
   3) l'information

c) Si je décide d'acheter un appareil-photo, le choix du produit est une opération difficile. La publicité la complique.
   1) l'appareil-photo
   2) le choix du produit
   3) l'opération difficile

d) La publicité lutte contre le complexe d'infériorité de l'individu qui n'a pas d'argent à gaspiller, afin de lui faire croire qu'il peut acquérir à peu près n'importe quoi.

1) le complexe d'infériorité
2) l'individu
3) l'argent

(The following sentences are taken from the passage you just read. Can you identify the noun or idea associated with the underlined pronoun?

a) Advertising is the composite of all the means used to acquaint the public with commercial products, to praise them, etc.

1) the means
2) the commercial products
3) the composite

b) The average man has a taste for information. For him it's both a curiosity and a need.

1) the average man
2) the taste
3) the information

c) If I decide to buy a camera, the choice of product is a difficult process. Advertising complicates it.

1) the camera
2) the choice of product
3) the process

d) Advertising counteracts the inferiority complex of the individual who does not have money to waste, in order to make him believe that he can acquire almost anything.

1) the inferiority complex
2) the individual
3) the money)

In an item such as this, the student is not only responsible for knowing which form of the object pronoun to use to replace a given noun, but also how that pronoun functions in the surrounding discourse to link ideas together. A similar type of item will be discussed in the section on writing and mixed-skills formats. (See pages 48-49.)

B. Recording Semantic Details

An example of a reading task that calls for discrete-point semantic choices is given below. This item also measures one aspect of discourse competence in that it involves reading a schedule rather than straight prose.

Sample 1.

Read the following excerpt from an airline brochure and answer the questions below in English.

Nous vous offrons les vols suivants au Québec:

Montréal: vol quotidien sans escale:
départ 12:00 arrivée 12:55

vol spécial "hommes d'affaires" lundi à vendredi sans escale:
départ 8:00 arrivée 8:55

Québec: sans escale: tous les jeudis, vendredis, samedis et dimanches
départ 14:30 arrivée 17:05

Ottawa-Hull: sans escale: tous les lundis, mercredis, jeudis et samedis
départ 10:30 arrivée 11:55

(We offer you the following flights to Quebec:

Montreal: daily non-stop flight:
leaves 12:00 arrives 12:55 p.m.

special businessman's flight Monday through Friday non-stop:
leaves 8:00 a.m. arrives 8:55 a.m.

Quebec: nonstop: every Thursday, Friday, Saturday, and Sunday
leaves 2:30 p.m. arrives 5:05 p.m.

Ottawa-Hull: nonstop: every Monday, Wednesday, Thursday, and Saturday
leaves 10:30 a.m. arrives 11:55 a.m.)

a) How many flights a week go to Montreal?
b) For whom is the 8 a.m. flight especially intended?
c) On what days of the week do the flights to Quebec City operate?

d) How many flights operate weekly to Hull?
e) Do any of the flights include a stopover en route?[16]

In this item, students have to locate the relevant semantic information within the discourse and make some inferences in order to interpret the schedule correctly.

C. Cloze Adaptation

Another example of a reading task that calls for discrete-point semantic-grammatical choices appears in Sample (1) below. The item actually combines reading comprehension with an indirect test of writing, since students are choosing the best "filler" for gaps in the discourse. This is a fairly commonly used variation of the cloze task; the advantage to this format is that students are not required to generate appropriate fillers for the slots from memory, but are only required to recognize them among the options given.

Sample 1.

"Les OVNI: visiteurs extra-terrestres?" (UFOs: Visitors from Outer Space?)

Choose the correct word from among the options given for each item below and mark the appropriate letter on your answer sheet.

La deuxième guerre mondiale a habitué l'espèce humaine à _____ les cieux plus attentivement que par le passé--soit avec	1.(a) observant (b) observer (c) observé
crainte, soit avec espoir--parce qu'à cette époque-là on ne _____ jamais ce qui pouvait apparaître au-dessus de sa tête.	2.(a) sait (b) connaît (c) savait (d) connaissait
En tout cas, c'est immédiatement après la fin de _____ guerre qu'ont commencé, puis se sont multipliées, les observations de	3.(a) ce (b) cette (c) cet
_____ nous appelons maintenant les OVNI (Objets Volants Non Identifiés), ou, en américain, les UFO....	4.(a) ce qui (b) ce que (c) ce dont
(The Second World War caused the human race to become accustomed to _____ at the heavens more attentively than in	1.(a) look (b) looked (c) looking

the past--either with fear or hope--because at that time you never _____ what might appear above your head.

2.a) know
b) become acquainted with
c) knew
d) become acquainted with

In any case, it was immediately after the end of _____ war that observations of

3.a) that (m)
b) that (f)
c) that (m)

_____ we now call UFOs (Unidentified Flying Objects) started, and then began to reoccur.)

4.a) which
b) what
c) of which

Obviously, one can choose to delete any set of discrete vocabulary or grammatical features of a text for testing purposes. One advantage to this format is that it serves to integrate into one unified context many points that teachers wish to test, allowing them to test those features operating "in concert," yet permitting discrete-point scoring procedures. Notice that all the decisions in this particular example can be made within the confines of a single sentence, or even within a phrase or "chunk" of the total discourse.[17]

These items, one might argue, therefore resemble traditional multiple-choice reading items in terms of the underlying task demands; that is, the items could be given in single-sentence frames just as easily as in larger contexts and still yield the same diagnostic information. The fundamental difference between the sample item given above and the discrete-point grammar tests of the past is that the sentences in which the slots appear follow one another logically and function together to form a unified narrative. If for no other reason than face validity, it seems far better to opt for a testing format in which the language of the test resembles "natural" language. The test then becomes much more reflective of course goals, even if the mechanics of the underlying discrete-point decisions remain essentially the same.

Another format that resembles this variation on the cloze test is illustrated below.

Sample 2.

Passé composé/imparfait. Choisissez et encerclez le verbe pour compléter chaque phrase.

Je me souviens des fêtes de Noël de mon enfance. Les souvenirs de cette fête célébrée en famille me sont toujours chers. D'habitude, nous (allions/sommes allés) en famille chez mes grands-parents. Malgré le fait qu'elle avait toujours détesté cuisiner, ma grand-mère (a préparé/préparait) un banquet royal. Mon grand-père, que nous (avons appellé/ appelions) "papa," (s'asseyait/s'est assis) cette fois-ci au bout de la table--siège d'autorité....

(Perfect/imperfect. Choose and circle the verb to complete each sentence.

I remember Christmas celebrations from my childhood. The memories of that celebration with the family are always dear to me. Usually, we (used to go/went) as a family to my grandparents' home. In spite of the fact that she had always hated cooking, my grandmother (prepared/used to prepare) a royal feast. My grandfather, whom we (called/used to call) "papa," (used to sit/sat) this time at the head of the table --the seat of authority....)[18]

One advantage to this format is that students do not have to look in the margins for appropriate fillers but can circle them within the passage. This may be less disruptive of the reading process, although no data have been collected to ascertain this as yet.

D. Comprehension Questions

Abundant examples of reading items using formats similar to listening formats (B), (C), and (D) mentioned earlier can be found in the testing literature of the past decade: that is, students must answer questions (in English) on a reading passage, summarize the main facts, or perform other follow-up tasks in English.

Several examples of more integrative reading comprehension tasks, in which skill in recognizing a paraphrase of a stimulus sentence is tested, have been discussed in Oller (1973). Oller's examples are not contextualized, but present the items in single sentence-length frames instead:

"Traditional" single-sentence item

Choose the sentence best expressing the meaning of the given sentence.

1. Helen's brother got married when she was eighteen years old.
   a) Helen's brother got married at the age of eighteen.
   b) Helen's brother was eighteen years old when she got married.
   c) When Helen was eighteen, her brother got married, etc.[19]

This item is followed by a similar one about Janet, who was watching her husband paint a chair.

In order to avoid the extremely piecemeal approach to language inherent in single sentence-length items of this type, and to further avoid the lack of logical continuation between items, it might be possible to adapt the paraphrasing idea to a more naturalistic language sample. If a whole paragraph were constructed around Helen's family, for example, the reading test might consist of an integral reading passage followed by a series of paraphrasing tasks based on its content. Each item following the passage could be constructed on the model suggested by Oller, but items would all relate to the original passage and would thus represent a more integrated language sample. An example of a contextualized adaptation of this format is given below.

Sample 1.

Read the following passage carefully. Then answer the multiple-choice questions, choosing the BEST summary of the information given in the passage.

Un marché de 250 millions d'habitants qui réunit dix pays qui pendant plus de dix siècles se sont fait la guerre: c'est le miracle moderne du Marché commun.

Il est né modestement après la deuxième guerre mondiale, à l'époque de la "guerre froide," du rapprochement des industries du charbon et de l'acier de six pays ex-belligérants (la France, l'Allemagne, l'Italie, la Belgique, la Hollande et le Luxembourg). Le charbon et l'acier étaient alors symboles de puissance militaire.

La seconde étape, celle de l'ouverture d'un Marché commun industriel et agricole, a coïncidé avec l'avènement en France de la Ve République, et l'arrivée au pouvoir du général de Gaulle. Beaucoup ont pensé alors que la réalisation du Marché commun serait incompatible avec les objectifs de de Gaulle, ...mais quand il a accordé l'indépendance aux anciennes colonies (notamment à l'Algérie), le général de Gaulle ramenait en fait la France en Europe.

Depuis lors, les six sont devenus les dix; la Grande-Bretagne, le Danemark, l'Irlande et récemment la Grèce sont devenus membres. Cela n'a d'ailleurs pas simplifié les problèmes qui se posent aux membres du Marché commun (politique commerciale, organisation de la production agricole) mais ce sont des problèmes essentiellement économiques. L'espoir belliqueux a entièrement disparu de l'Europe occidentale....

(A marketplace for 250 million inhabitants that reunites ten countries who, for more than ten centuries, were always at war: this is the miracle of the Common Market.

It had its modest beginnings after the Second World War, at the time of the "Cold War," as a result of the union of the coal and steel industries of six countries that were former enemies [France, Germany, Italy, Belgium, Holland, and Luxembourg]. Coal and steel were symbols of military power at that time.

The second stage, that of the opening of a common industrial and agricultural market, coincided with the beginning of the Fifth Republic in France and the arrival to power of General de Gaulle. A lot of people thought then that the realization of the Common Market would be incompatible with de Gaulle's objectives,...but when he gave the former colonies [notably Algeria] their independence, General de Gaulle brought France effectively back into the European community.

From then on, the six became the ten: Great Britain, Denmark, Ireland, and recently, Greece have become members. This has not, however, simplified the problems that Common Market countries are experiencing (the politics of business, organization of agricultural production), but these are essentially economic problems. The desire for war has completely disappeared from Western Europe....)

Choose the statements from each group of sentences below that state the information in the passage most correctly.

a) 1) The miracle of the Common Market is that there are 250 million members.
   2) The Common Market has lasted despite many years of war among its members.
   3) The Common Market brings together ten countries who have had many political differences over the centuries.

b) 1) The Common Market was created during the Second World War.
   2) Six countries that had been enemies during World War II created the Common Market after the war.
   3) The Common Market is a symbol of united military and industrial power.

c) 1) It was coincidental that the Common Market was created at the same time as the Fifth Republic in France.
   2) A second stage of the development of the Common Market coincided with the assumption of power in France by de Gaulle.
   3) De Gaulle wanted to include Algeria, newly independent of colonial rule, in the Common Market countries.

d) 1) Four new countries have been added to the Common Market since its creation.

2) The addition of new countries to the Common Market has simplified some of the problems relating to the economy in Europe.
3) Western Europe has lost all hope of solving its economic problems, even with the advent of the Common Market.[20]

E. Logical Continuation Items

Another integrative reading item format is the "logical continuation" item, in which a paragraph-length context is provided, followed by a series of multiple-choice options, one of which follows logically and completes the thought of the paragraph. The most logical completion can be chosen only when students have thorougly understood the preceding context.

A related integrative reading comprehension format consists of a set of sentences, all of which go together logically except for one. Students cross out the sentence that does not belong in the total context.

Sample 1.

In the story below, cross out the sentence in each paragraph that does not fit the context. There is one extraneous sentence per paragraph.

"Tout a commencé à bord de mon avion personnel, en route pour Yakima, Washington. J'ai reçu une communication qu'un avion de l'U.S. Navy avait disparu une heure plus tôt dans la région. Cette région des Etats-Unis est une des plus belles que j'ai jamais vues. Je me suis détourné de ma route pour participer à la recherche.

Soudain, j'ai vu une lueur aveuglante qui se reflétait sur mon avion. En cherchant la cause, j'ai regardé autour de moi et j'ai découvert sur ma gauche une formation de neuf objets volants. Le vol devient difficile s'il y a beaucoup de vent. La vitesse de ces machines et leur mode de déplacement m'ont vraiment étonné...."

(Everything started aboard my private plane, en route to Yakima, Washington. I received a radio message that a U.S. Navy plane had disappeared an hour earlier in the region. This region of the United States is one of the most beautiful I've ever seen. I turned off my route to help in the search.

Suddenly, I saw a blinding light reflecting off my plane. While searching for the origin of the light, I looked around me and discovered on my left a formation of nine flying objects. Flight becomes difficult when there's a lot of wind. The speed of these machines and their method of travel really surprised me....)

F. Native-Language/Second-Language Summary

Comprehension items that require synthesis of various facts into an integral passage can be developed using formats similar to listening formats (D) and (E), explained earlier (i.e., a passage is read and the student writes an English-language summary, chooses a title, creates or chooses a "title" or "moral" of a story, or classifies the passage globally in some way). Some good examples can be found in the sources cited earlier.

Sample 1.

Lisez le paragraphe et choisissez la phrase qui représente le mieux l'idée principale.

Quand on revient d'un séjour dans un pays étranger, la première chose dont on parle est presque toujours la cuisine: non seulement la nourriture mais aussi la façon de la préparer, de la manger, les heures des repas, tous les rites qui les accompagnent et qui caractérisent les gens du pays mieux que n'importe quel autre aspect de la vie.

a) La nourriture est la première chose qu'on remarque pendant un séjour à l'étranger.
b) La cuisine d'un pays étranger est si remarquable que tout le monde en parle dès son retour à son pays natal.
c) La cuisine, la façon dont on la prépare, et les rites qui accompagnent les repas caractérisent un peuple mieux que tout autre aspect de la vie quotidienne.
d) La façon dont on prépare la nourriture et les coutumes qui accompagnent les repas sont beaucoup plus importantes dans les pays étrangers que chez nous.

(Read the paragraph and choose the sentence that best represents the main idea.

When one returns from a stay in a foreign country, the first thing one talks about is almost always the food: not only the food itself, but also the way it's prepared, the way it's eaten, the meal hours--all the rites that accompany eating and that characterize the people of the country better than almost any other aspect of their lives.

a) Food is the first thing one notices during a stay in a foreign country.
b) The cooking in a foreign country is so remarkable that everyone talks about it on his return to his native country.
c) Cooking, the way that food is prepared, and the rituals accompanying the meals characterize a people better than any other aspect of their daily life.

d) The way food is prepared and the rituals accompanying meals are much more important in foreign countries than here.)[21]

In writing items of this type, care must be taken that each distractor is plausible to students who have only partially understood the passage; only one answer should be clearly correct. Note, in the example above, how elements of the passage have been worked into the distractors and will make sense to students who have not comprehended the passage in its entirety. One negative factor in multiple-choice testing, of course, is that items can be successfully answered by chance. To avoid this, other item formats may be preferable. In any case, teachers will need considerable practice in writing integrative comprehension items of this type, and any items they write should be submitted to item analysis as well as to "pilot" testing by colleagues and/ or native speakers.

G. Global Classification

An example of an elementary-level reading item requiring an inferential, global response is the following:

Sample 1.

Grand-mère Laforge is the local "Ann Landers" columnist for a town's French-language newspaper. You read the following letter from one of her readers:

Chère grand-mère Laforge,
J'ai presque quatorze ans. L'année dernière, pendant les vacances de Noël, j'ai recontré un garçon très sympathique. Nous sommes sortis ensemble mais mes parents pensent que je suis trop jeune pour sortir avec un garçon. Nous sommes tous les deux malheureux. Qu'est-ce que je peux faire pour être heureuse?

(Dear Grandmother Laforge,
I'm almost fourteen. Last year during Christmas vacation I met a really nice boy. We went out together but my parents think I'm too young to go out with a boy. We're both unhappy. What can I do to be happy?)

Which of the following answers do you think Grand-mère Laforge would write?

a) Il ne faut pas aller en vacances.
b) Il ne faut pas présenter le garçon à tes parents.
c) Il faut être malheureux.
d) Il faut présenter le garçon à tes parents.

Circle the letter beside the correct answer.

a) You shouldn't go on vacations.
b) Don't introduce this boy to your parents.
c) You have to be unhappy.
d) You ought to introduce this boy to your parents.)[22]

H. Identifying Sociolinguistic Factors

A similar item with a sociolinguistic focus follows:

Sample 1.

Read the following conversation and the question below. Then circle the letter beside the correct answer on this page.

A: Allo?
B: Bonjour, c'est Louis. Normand est la?
A: Non, pas encore. Veux-tu lui laisser un message?
B: Vous ne savez pas a quelle heure il va rentrer?
A: Non, je ne sais pas.
B: Ben...dites-lui que j'ai appele, s'il vous plait.
A: D'accord, Louis.
B: Merci. Bonjour.
A: Bonjour.

(A: Hello?
B: Hello, this is Louis. Is Norman there?
A: No, not yet. Do you [familiar] want to leave a message for him?
B: You [formal] don't know what time he's coming back?
A: No, I don't.
B: Well...tell [formal] him that I called, please.
A: All right, Louis.
B: Thank you. Goodbye.
A: Goodbye.)[23]

What can we guess about the speakers, from the way they are talking to each other?

a) The speakers are friends of about the same age.
b) Louis is probably speaking with Normand's younger sister.
c) Louis is probably much younger than the other speaker.
d) Louis probably calls the other speaker by her first name.

To combine a global reading comprehension task with a test of cultural sensitivity, a cultural assimilator or minidrama might be used. Good ideas for items of this type can be found in Bee and D'Alleva (1977), Levno (1977), Shiver (1977), and Snyder

(1977), for Italian, French, German, and Spanish, respectively. An item in Italian is given below.

Sample 2.

"Giorno di festa." È il 4 ottobre. Assisi, Italia.

Frank: Perbacco, quante luci. Ma è sempre così illuminata questa città?

Margherita: Oh, no, oggi è il 4 ottobre e qui è giorno di gran festa.

Frank: A proposito di festa, Carlotta e Marco dicono che si balla in casa di Francesco stasera.

Carlotta: Si balla, e come! Si cena e ci sarà anche tanto spumante. Canteremo e danzeremo fino a tardi.

Frank: Ma qual'è l'occasione? È forse il compleanno di Francesco?

Carlotta: No, non si tratta del compleanno: oggi è il suo onomastico. (guardando Frank) Veramente è anche il tuo.

Frank: Il mio...che?

Di sera in casa di Francesco:

Margherita: Ciao Francesco e auguri.
Carlotta: Sei festeggiatissimo!
Marco: Auguri, auguri!
Francesco: Grazie, grazie, ma dobbiamo fare gli auguri anche a Frank.
Tutti: Accipicchia, sei capitato a proposito, Frank!
Frank: (Meravigliato) Ma cosa succede?

("Holiday." It's October 4th. Assisi, Italy.

Frank: Gosh! What a lot of lights. But is this city always lit up like this?

Margherita: Oh, no. Today's October 4th and this is a big holiday.

Frank: Speaking of holidays, Charlotte and Mark said we're going to dance at Francesco's house tonight.

Carlotta: We're going to dance, and how! We're going to have dinner and there will be a lot of champagne. We're going to sing and dance all night.

Frank: But what's the occasion? Is this maybe Francesco's birthday?

Carlotta: No, it's not a question of birthdays: today is his Saint's day. [Looking at Frank] Really, it's yours, too.

Frank: Mine...my what?

That evening at Francesco's house:

Margherita:	Hi, Francesco, and best wishes.
Carlotta:	This is quite a celebration!
Marco:	Best wishes!
Francesco:	Thank you, thank you, but we have to extend best wishes also to Frank.
Everyone:	Good lord! You really turned up at the right moment, Frank.
Frank:	[Very surprised] What's going on?)

<u>Why is Frank confused about the celebration?</u>

a) Italians celebrate their Saint's day more than their birthday.
b) It is election time, and the city is lighted.
c) St. Francis is the patron of Assisi, and October 4th is dedicated to him.
d) Francesco is giving a party in honor of Frank's arrival.[24]

[*Editor's note:* The English equivalent of Francesco is Frank or Francis.]

Reading comprehension items can be generated from many sources available to the teacher: adaptations can be made of existing supplementary text materials, readers, or other edited texts suitable to the level of the learner. Teachers can generate their own short texts as well. Ideas for creating reading items as well as listening, writing, and mixed skills items will be presented.

III. CONTEXTUALIZED WRITING AND MIXED SKILLS FORMATS

A. Controlled (Guided) Compositions

Since global writing tasks are not as difficult to contextualize as the more discrete-point item formats, they will be treated first in this section. Some very fine ideas for testing global skills via writing have been described in the sources cited previously under listening and reading items. Controlled or guided compositions, where students respond to question prods, pictorial or verbal cues, or other similar guidelines, have been used in the past as tests of communicative ability, using writing as the test medium. (That is, the items that follow are not necessarily tests of writing in terms of expository writing in the target language, but rather they use writing as a medium for testing such aspects of the developing language as grammar and vocabulary.)

Sample 1. (Spanish)

You are writing to a friend in Spain, and this person wants to know all about North American customs. In his or her last letter, your Spanish friend asked you about holidays in the U.S. and how they are celebrated. You want to describe at least four holidays--their dates, what they are called, and how your family celebrates them. Be sure to use vocabulary from "el calendario" in your letter.[25]

Sample 2.

Racontez une histoire originale au passé. Utilisez les questions suivantes comme guide, et attention au choix entre l'imparfait et le passé composé!

a) Dans votre histoire, quel est le mois?
b) Quelle heure est-il?
c) Quel temps fait-il? Où êtes-vous? Avec qui?
d) Qui arrive sur la scène? Décrivez la personne.
e) Que fait cette personne? Que faites-vous? Comment réagit votre camarade?
f) Racontez la fin de votre histoire.

(Tell an original story in the past. Use the following questions as a guide, and be careful of the choice you make between the imparfait and the passé composé.

a) In your story, what month is it?
b) What time is it?
c) What's the weather like? Where are you? With whom?

d) Who arrives on the scene? Describe this person.
e) What's this person doing? What are you doing? How does your friend react?
f) Describe the ending to your story.)[26]

Both the global writing tasks in the examples given above will elicit certain features of the language that are related to specified course goals: in the Spanish example, dates and holidays will emerge in the students' discussions of the topic provided; in the French example, times, weather conditions, descriptive adjectives, and actions in the past will be elicited. These items will still be somewhat difficult to score, however. As Bartz (1976) points out, "tests of communicative competence involving writing are somewhat more difficult to score and involve a great deal more subjectivity on the part of the scorer" (p. 59).

To overcome this problem, Bartz and others have presented some fairly objective scoring methods for these types of tests. One possibility is to assign a global score to a written language sample on the basis of weighted subratings: factors such as comprehensibility, ease of expression, cohesion and coherence, linguistic accuracy, breadth and appropriateness of vocabulary, and the like could be judged and rated globally (from A to E/F) and transformed into numerical scores. (See Figures 3 and 4, which are oral test scoresheets, for ideas for such a rating system.) Although one can limit the writing task somewhat in global composition tests, it is still difficult to elicit all the discrete items one might be interested in for achievement testing purposes. In order to supplement these general achievement tests, which might be administered periodically during the course of a semester or school year, the following contextualized writing and mixed-skills formats are suggested to allow for the testing of vocabulary and grammar on hourly exams and quizzes.

B. Sentence Cues (Writing)

Items of this type consist of "telegraphic" or "slash" sentences: sentence elements are provided as the stimulus and the student must combine them into complete and meaningful sentences, adding any necessary function words and making any necessary morphological changes. To contextualize this type of format, each individual stimulus should be connected to the others in the subsection of the test, either in a logical sequence or in some thematic sense.

Sample 1.

You are a journalist who has just interviewed a witness of a UFO incident. The notes you made during the interview are given below. Write out your report in complete sentences, using the past tense whenever appropriate.

NOTES

Kenneth Arnold, in personal plane, 6/14/47, around 6 p.m. Gets radio message--U.S. Navy planes missing. Decides to participate in search. Suddenly sees blinding light reflected off plane--looks around for source--sees 9 flying objects, flying in formation on left....

Sample 2.

Françoise is a politically active student who is participating in a feminist demonstration in Paris. Using the words and phrases provided, recreate her opinions.

a) Il/être/essentiel/femmes/être/unifié
b) Il faut/plus/femmes/savoir/que/il y avoir/manifestation/aujourd'hui
c) Je/penser/Mitterrand/pouvoir/améliorer/qualité de vie/pour/femmes/français
d) Ce/année/il/ne pas être/possible/que/femmes/gagner/autant/argent/que/hommes....

(a) It/to be/essential/women/to be/unified
b) It is necessary/more/women/to know/that/there to be/demonstration/today
c) I/to think/Mitterand/to be able/to better/quality of life/for/women/French
d) This/year/it/not to be/possible/that/women/to earn/as much/money/as/men.)

C. Contextualized Partial Translation (Reading/Writing)

Valette (1977) presents this item type in her text on testing, but she illustrates it with single-sentence frames. A contextualized, connected version of several paragraphs in length can be created quite easily if all the sentences follow one another logically in a conversation or narrative. Two examples of partial translations are given below. The second of the two formats, which resembles a cloze-type task, seems to be less disruptive of the natural flow of the discourse.

Sample 1.

Complete the conversation in Spanish, using the English sentence equivalents as your guide.

Paco: __________, Juan. Busco por todas partes mi librito __________ tiene todos los números de teléfono de las chicas __________, pero __________. (Good grief, Juan. I'm looking all over for my little black book that has all of the phone numbers of the girls I know, but I can't find it.)

Juan: Si tu no tienes una chica __________ ir a la fiesta, tengo un amigo __________ hermana quiere ir. (If you don't have a girl to go with to the party, I have a friend whose sister wants to go.)

Paco: ¿Tienes su número de teléfono? (Do you have her phone number?)

Juan: __________ el número ahora pero voy a __________ para __________. (I don't remember the number now, but I'm going to ask my friend for it for you.)[27]

Sample 2.

Margot et Annick, sa camarade de chambre, détestent leur appartement. Un jour elles décident de chercher un autre logement. Complétez leur conversation. La conversation en anglais est à côté de la conversation en français.

(Margot and Annick, her roommate, hate their apartment. One day they decide to look for other lodgings. Complete their conversation. The English conversation is next to the French conversation.)

Annick: Je n'aime pas _____ appartement. La cuisine est trop _____ et _____. En plus, c'est trop cher!	I don't like our apartment. The kitchen is too small, and there's no garden. Besides, it's too expensive!
Margot: _____ un appartement à louer près de l'université?	Doesn't your aunt have an apartment for rent near the university?
Annick: Ah oui! __________! Je vais _____ téléphoner tout de suite!...	Ah yes! That's true! I'm going to phone her right away!...

One advantage of the partial translation format is that the teacher can test a variety of discrete points of vocabulary and grammar efficiently in one single subsection of the test, and the items, though scored in a discrete-point fashion, are still embedded in naturalistic discourse. Because grammar and vocabulary must be recalled, the test items are also diagnostic. One disadvantage of the first of the two formats is the need to insert native-language equivalents into the passage, which interrupts its natural flow.

D. Modifications of the Cloze Test: Gap-Filling Items (Reading/Writing)

Cloze tests have been the subject of much discussion and controversy recently; one problem associated with this type of test is the rather arbitrary nature of the deletions when an "every-*n*th-word" procedure is used, and the negative reaction of many students to exact-word scoring procedures or to the test in general (Shohamy 1982). To adapt the cloze-type format successfully to foreign language classroom tests, some alternatives are suggested below.

1. Non-arbitrary deletion procedures. Specific parts of speech are chosen to be deleted from a passage and may be presented in a list in alphabetical order before the passage, after it, or in a box beside the text itself. If verbs are deleted, students must choose the verb that fits the context semantically, conjugate it appropriately, and pay attention to tense. Students must make all morphological changes necessary for other parts of speech deleted as well (such as adjectives, articles, possessive pronouns).

Sample (a)

Marie and Jeanne are talking on the phone. Complete the conversation by choosing the appropriate verb from the box on the right. Each verb should be used only once per section. Be sure to make a sensible choice of the verb and to use the form and tense that are most appropriate to the context.

devoir lire vouloir

Jeanne: Allô, Marie? Comment vas-tu? Je te téléphone parce que je _____ te parler.

Marie: Est-ce que tu _____ l'annonce dans le journal hier soir?

Jeanne: Oui, c'est justement pour cela que je te téléphone. Je n(e) _____ pas rater mon examen d'anglais. Ecoute, vas-tu m'aider à étudier?

Marie: D'accord, mais tu me donneras 50 francs dès que tu _____ le résultat.

Jeanne: J(e) _____ que c'est un peu cher. Je n(e) _____ pas payer plus de 30 francs.

voir
pouvoir
croire

Marie: C'est assez. On se _____ demain, alors.

Jeanne: Oui, nous _____ ensemble tout le texte quand tu arriveras.

lire
croire
pouvoir
voir

Marie: D'accord. Prépare aussi une composition. Je la corrigerai demain.

Jeanne: Merci, Marie, je _____ que tu es un bon prof. Si je réussis à mon examen, je te ferai un beau cadeau.

Marie: Quand tu réussiras à ton examen, tu _____ aller en Angleterre pour pratiquer ton anglais!

(Jeanne: Hello, Marie? How are you? I'm calling you because I _____ talk to you.

to have to
to read
to want to

Marie: Did you _____ the ad in the paper last night?

Jeanne: Yes, that's exactly why I'm calling you. I don't _____ fail my English test. Listen, can you help me study?

Marie: OK, but you'll pay me 50 francs as soon as you _____ the results.

Jeanne: I _____ that's a little expensive. I _____ not pay more than 30 francs.

to see
to be able to
to believe/
to think

Marie: That's all right. We'll _____ each other tomorrow, then.

Jeanne: Yes, we'll _____ the whole text together when you get here.

Marie: OK. Prepare a composition, too. I'll correct it tomorrow.

Jeanne: Thanks, Marie, I _____ you're a good teacher. If I pass my exam, I'll get you a nice gift.

Marie: When you pass your test, you _____ to go to England to practice your English!)

to read to believe/ to think to be able to to see

Sample (b)

Complétez le texte suivant en choisissant l'expression qui convient parmi les mots encadrés, à droite.

M. Durand, l'homme _____ je parle, est médecin. Il travaille beaucoup avec les gens qui ont besoin de lui. Il leur ordonne des médicaments, _____ est normal, étant donné son métier. M. Durand rend souvent visite à ses malades, chez _____ il trouve toujours une bonne tasse de thé. Parfois, il travaille à l'hôpital _____ il guérit ses malades avec l'aide des infirmières. M. Durand est un homme très gentil _____ j'admire beaucoup.

ce qui ce que ce dont dont lequel de laquelle qui que où

(Complete the following text by choosing the most appropriate words from the box to the right.

Mr. Durand, the man _____ I'm talking, is a doctor. He works a lot with people who need him. He prescribes medicine for _____, often visits his patients, at _____ homes he always finds a nice cup of tea. Sometimes he works at the hospital _____ he cures his patients with the help of the nurses. Mr. Durand is a very nice man _____ I admire a lot.)

what which who about whom whom them whose where

The example in German below includes a small sketch to make more precise the choice of preposition to be made by first-year high school students.

Sample (c)

Fill in the description of Oliver's house below, using the appropriate preposition from the box on the right and adding the appropriate article in the second blank before each noun. Refer to the sketch to make sure you are using the correct preposition. Prepositions may be used more than once.

Olivers Haus steht _____ _____ Ecke Bauerstraße. Es ist ein großes Haus mit drei Stockwerken. _____ _____ Haus ist die Garage. Das Auto steht _____ _____ Garage. Der Garten ist _____ _____ Haus. Am Zaun, _____ _____ Gartentür, hängt das Schild. Der Dachboden ist _____ _____ Wohnung. Wenn es regnet, hängt Olivers Mutter die Wäsche _____ _____ Boden.

an
auf
hinter
in
neben
über

(Oliver's house is _____ the corner of Bauer Street. It's a big house with three stories. _____ the house is the garage. The car is _____ the garage. The garden is _____ the house. On the fence, _____ the garden gate, hangs a sign. The attic is _____ the living quarters. When it rains, Oliver's mother hangs the wash _____ the attic.)[28]

on
over
above
behind
in
next to

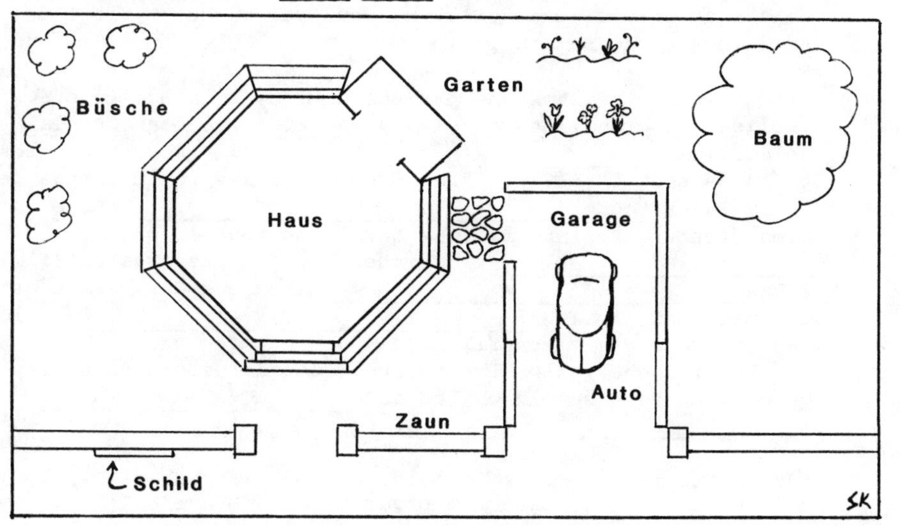

2. Multiple-choice cues. A modified cloze passage is presented to students in which gaps in the discourse are accompanied by multiple-choice options below the text, within the text, or beside the slots in the margin. (See pp. 29 and 30 for examples of two possible formats.)

E. Discourse Transformation

In order to test discourse competence in conjunction with grammatical competence, teachers can design test items in which students transform the discourse in some way, using specific grammatical features recently studied.

1. Direct object pronouns. The following item requires elementary French students to modify an original passage by using direct object pronouns for any repeated nouns, which results in a much more cohesive and less stilted text.

Sample (a)

(Original Passage): Jeannette aime beaucoup la télévision. Elle regarde la télévision tout le temps. Ses programmes préférés sont "M*A*S*H," "Lou Grant," et les rediffusions (reruns) de "Mary Tyler Moore." Elle regarde ces programmes le lundi. Elle aime écouter les informations aussi, surtout le matin. Elle écoute les informations de la chaîne 8, d'habitude. Maintenant, elle regarde un film. Elle aime beaucoup le film parce que Cary Grant est l'acteur principal. Elle adore Cary Grant, et elle regarde tous ses vieux films.

Le dimanche, elle aime regarder les émissions spéciales qu'on peut voir sur la chaîne 12. Elle va regarder ces émissions ce week-end. Elle ne veut pas manquer (miss) ces émissions cette semaine.

Directives. Refaites les phrases où il y a un nom répété. Utilisez un pronom convenable. Jeannette aime beaucoup la télévision. ______________________________. Ses programmes préférés sont "M*A*S*H," "Lou Grant," et les rediffusions de "Mary Tyler Moore." ____________________________. Elle aime écouter les informations aussi, surtout le matin. _______________________. Maintenant, elle regarde un film. Elle ______________________________ parce que Cary Grant est l'acteur principal. ______________________________, et elle regarde tous ses vieux films.

Le dimanche, elle aime regarder les émissions spéciales qu'on peut voir sur la chaîne 12. ________________________. ______________________________.

(Jeannette really likes television. She watches television all the time. Her favorite programs are "M*A*S*H," "Lou

Grant," and "Mary Tyler Moore" reruns. She watches these programs on Mondays. She likes to listen to the news, too, especially in the morning. She listens to the news on channel 8, usually. Now she's watching a movie. She likes the movie a lot because Cary Grant is the leading actor. She adores Cary Grant, and she watches all of his old films.

On Sundays, she likes to watch special programs that you can see on channel 12. She's going to watch these programs this weekend. She doesn't want to miss these programs this week.

Directions: Redo the sentences where there is a repeated noun. Use the appropriate object pronoun. Jeannette really likes television. ______________________. Her favorite programs are "M*A*S*H," "Lou Grant," and "Mary Tyler Moore" reruns. ______________________. She likes to listen to the news, too, especially in the morning. ______________________. Now she's watching a movie. ______________________ because Cary Grant is the leading actor. ______________________, and she watches all of his old films.

On Sundays, she likes to watch special programs that you can see on Channel 12. ______________________. ______________________.)

2. <u>Elaboration with adverbs</u>. In this test item, students are first required to convert adjectives to adverbs and then, reading the passage, choose an appropriate adverb for each slot in the discourse, making certain the adverb makes sense.

<u>Sample (a)</u>

<u>Liste des adjectifs à transformer en adverbes</u>: bref, final, gentil, immédiat, lent, malheureux, poli, rapide, vain, violent

Rendez cette histoire plus vivante en substituant à chaque adjectif proposé l'adverbe correspondant qui convient pour le contexte. Le premier tiret est rempli pour servir comme exemple.

L'Inspecteur s'est <u>finalement</u> endormi à minuit. Mais, _____ le téléphone a sonné _____ à deux heures du matin. Le détective a essayé _____ de trouver le récepteur. Il l'a décroché _____ et a dit "Allô?" Une voix de femme a répondu _____ avec des mots qu'il ne comprenait pas _____. "Répétez _____, s'il vous plaît, Madame" a-t-il demandé _____. "Il est mort" a dit _____ la dame. "Qui?" a-t-il démandé _____. "Mon chien. N'êtes-vous pas monsieur le vétérinaire?"

(List of adjectives to change to adverbs: brief, final, gentle, immediate, slow, polite, rapid, vain, violent

Make this story more lively by using adverbs in the slots; use adverbs that correspond to the adjectives above.

The telephone rang _____ at two o'clock in the morning. The detective tried _____ to find the receiver. He took it off the hook _____ and said "Hello?" A woman's voice answered _____ in words that he wasn't able to understand _____. "Would you please say that again _____, madame?" he asked _____. "He's dead," said the woman, _____. "Who?" he asked _____. "My dog. Aren't you the veterinarian?")[29]

In this example, various adverbs could be used in some of the blanks and still make sense, although they would flavor the story differently. Credit should be given for <u>any</u> acceptable adverb given. This particular item combines reading comprehension, discourse competence, and grammatical competence and should be scored accordingly. (Partial credit should be given for correct forms, even though correct fit is not achieved, and vice-versa.) One solution is to put the adjectives to be transformed next to the blanks where they belong. This changes the nature of the item, however, reducing it to a grammatical task embedded within the discourse. The teacher should decide which competencies to tap when choosing among possible formats and should score the item accordingly.

3. <u>Elaboration with relative clauses</u>. In this type of item, students learn to write more cohesive discourse via relative clause constructions. One possibility is to give the students a very simplistic narrative passage, perhaps a paragraph long, in which asterisks are inserted wherever a relative clause could be added. (Any elaborative mechanism could be tested in this manner: students could be asked to add adjectives, adverbs, connectors, and the like, depending on the grammatical category that the teacher wishes to test.) If students are responsible for adding relative clauses of their own invention, this item becomes a creative writing item as well, allowing for divergent answers. One way to limit the possibilities (i.e., test for <u>convergent</u> answers) is to set the task up in the following way:

<u>Sample (a)</u>

Link the two phrases in each section of the narrative below with a relative pronoun. The symbol * indicates the beginning of the relative clause.

1. Je vais prendre des vacances. *J'ai vraiment besoin de vacances. 2. Ma camarade de chambre* vient avec moi. Le nom de ma camarade de chambre est Elise. 3. Elise a une nouvelle voiture. *Elle a acheté sa voiture en février. 4. Nous allons à Neuchâtel. *Les parents d'Elise ont une maison à Neuchâtel. 5. Le père d'Elise* nous a invitées. Elise a téléphoné à son père la semaine dernière....

(1. I'm going to go on vacation. *I really need a vacation. 2. My roommate* is coming with me. My roommate's name is Elise. 3. Elise has a new car. *She bought her car in February. 4. We're going to Neuchâtel. *Elise's parents have a house in Neuchâtel. 5. Elise's father* invited us. Elise called her father last week....)[30]

The example above eliminates the need for students to add relative clauses on their own. For this reason, it is perhaps better suited for discrete-point, diagnostic testing than is the creative version mentioned earlier. However, the creative writing task, in which students invent their own elaborative clauses, constitutes a better global writing task, since discourse competence is coupled with grammatical competence. Such tasks may be reserved for a general achievement test or a final exam.

4. Partial conversations (reading/writing). A somewhat more creative writing item is one in which students read half a conversation and are asked to supply a logical "other half," imagining, for example, what a person on the other end of a phone line must have been saying. This format is especially useful for testing question formation, or, more specifically, testing interrogative pronouns, adjectives, or adverbs.

Sample (a)

Imaginez l'autre partie de la conversation au téléphone. Quelles sonts les questions posées? Les mots soulignés indiquent la réponse à la question imaginaire.

Jean-Luc: Allô?
Marie-Eve: ______________________________?
Jean-Luc: Robert? Non, il n'est pas ici.
Marie-Eve: ______________________________?
Jean-Luc: Il est à la bibliothèque ce soir.
Marie-Eve: ______________________________?
Jean-Luc: Je crois qu'il étudie pour son examen d'histoire.
Marie-Eve: ______________________________?
Jean-Luc: Probablement vers 11 heures. Je lui dirai que tu as téléphoné, d'accord?... Au revoir, Marie-Eve.

(Imagine the other part of the telephone conversation below. What are the questions asked? The underlined words indicate the answer to the imaginary question.

Jean-Luc: Hello?
Marie-Eve: ________________________________?
Jean-Luc: Robert? No, he's not here.
Marie-Eve: ________________________________?
Jean-Luc: He's at the library this evening.
Marie-Eve: ________________________________?
Jean-Luc: I think he's studying for his history test.
Marie-Eve: ________________________________?
Jean-Luc: Probably around 11 o'clock. I'll tell him you called, OK? Bye, Marie-Eve.)

A less convergent item, in which many questions might be possible, is given below.

Sample (b)

Voici quelques réponses aux questions posées par le frère de Jean-Paul, qui lui rend visite à l'université. Inventez des questions avec des expressions interrogatives.

(1) ________________________?
C'est une revue française.
(2) ________________________?
A l'université.
(3) ________________________?
Jacqueline.

(Here are a few answers to questions asked by Jean-Paul's brother, who's visiting him at the university. Invent some possible question using interrogative expressions you know.

(1) ________________________?
It's a French magazine.
(2) ________________________?
At the university.
(3) ________________________?
Jacqueline.)[31]

5. Eliciting appropriate questions. Another way to elicit interrogative words and expressions is to provide a series of statements in which certain words have been left out. Students must ask an appropriate question to find out what those missing elements are. The example below asks students to imagine that they are listening to a radio broadcast during an electrical storm, and that static interrupts the broadcast whenever they see the symbol ///.

Sample (a)

Une soirée orageuse, vous écoutez une émission à la radio sur la santé et la grande forme. Mais il y a beaucoup de parasites (static) et il est difficile d'entendre tous les mots. Voici quelques extraits du programme. Quelles questions devez-vous poser pour savoir ce que le speaker a dit?

Modèle: "Pendant notre dernière émission, /// nous a conseillé de faire plus de promenades." Vous dites: "Qui nous a conseillé de faire plus de promenades?"

(1) "Pour être en grande forme, on doit /// tous les jours."
(2) "Pour éviter les problèmes digestifs, /// est hautement recommandé."
(3) "La nuit, quand vous ne pouvez pas dormir, vous pouvez toujours compter sur ///."

(One stormy night, you're listening to a radio program on health and fitness. But there is a lot of static and it's hard to hear all the words. Here are some excerpts from the program. What questions do you have to ask to find out what the speaker said?

Model: "During our last program, /// advised us to take more walks." You say, "Who advised us to take more walks?"

(1) "To be in good shape, you have to /// every day."
(2) "To avoid digestive problems, /// is highly recommended."
(3) "At night, when you can't sleep, you can always count on ///.")

F. Information Gaps (Listening/Writing)

A combination of listening and writing items that resembles the real-world tasks of note taking and interviewing can be achieved by the integrative format described below. Students listen to a short account of an incident and fill out a form on their test papers, much as they would do for the listening items described under Sample 2 on pages 15-17. In this task, however, some of the information requested on the form is not given in the passage. After hearing the passage twice, students must devise a series of questions that would elicit the missing information they need for the form.

Sample 1.

Interview between a journalist and a witness to a UFO incident. (English is used here for purposes of illustration, but the passage, which is to be read twice to students, would be in the target language.)

Journalist: What is your name, sir?
Witness: Kenneth Arnold.
Journalist: What happened, exactly?
Witness: I was flying in my personal plane on my way to Phoenix. All of a sudden, I saw a blinding light reflected off my plane. I looked around, and on my left I saw a formation of nine flying objects.
Journalist: Are you sure they weren't just airplanes?
Witness: No, they moved too fast and they were shaped like saucers.
Journalist: What did you do?
Witness: I put out an alert to other planes in the region over my radio.

Student Information Sheet: Fill in the information needed below as you listen to the passage. You will hear the passage twice. There are some items on your form for which no information is given. After you have filled in all the facts you hear, design appropriate questions to get the rest of the information you need.

Witness's name ______________________________
Witness's occupation ______________________________
Location of witness at time of incident ____________________
Date and time of incident ______________________________
Number of objects sighted ______________________________
Color of objects ______________________________
Shape of objects ______________________________
Witness's first thoughts on seeing the objects ____________
____
Additional questions you need to ask:
____
____
____
____

In scoring an item such as this, it is important to avoid "double jeopardy": points can be awarded for all the facts taken down from the listening passage and additional points for each appropriate question asked in the follow-up task. If a student did not hear a piece of information that <u>was</u> provided in the passage, but did ask an appropriate question to elicit that information, partial credit can be given. Because this item is integrative in nature, and success in the second task is somewhat dependent on success in the first task, it is important to devise a scoring procedure that does not penalize the student too harshly for missed information, and that does award credit for efforts to compensate for that part of the test item missed. The nature of this item is such that a student who understood very little of the passage could still gain points on the follow-up task, since it is clear from the Student Information Sheet what questions need to be asked, and points can be awarded for any appropriate question formulated by the student.

G. Logical Continuation (Listening/Speaking or Reading/Writing)

Another divergent-production item type that requires creative writing is the logical continuation item. Students read a short paragraph describing a situation. They are then required to write a one- or two-sentence logical continuation of the paragraph. They may, for example, write a concluding sentence or produce another sentence to carry the narrative on in some way. This item blends reading comprehension with creative writing (in order for students to produce a logical continuation, they must have understood the point of the preceding paragraph). The conclusion or continuation the students write can be scored in terms of its semantic and linguistic content: a coherent and appropriate conclusion that is faulty can be awarded partial credit; a correct sentence that does not follow the paragraph logically can also receive partial credit.

Howard (1980) gives an example of a logical continuation of a conversation in terms of its sociolinguistic appropriateness.

Sample 1.

> Consider the following: Un commis très obligeant à la réception de votre hôtel vous assure qu'une lettre attendue n'est pas arrivée. Vous désirez lui répondre poliment. Il vous dit: "Je regrette, Madame. Peut-être que cette lettre arrivera dans le courrier de l'après-midi." (A very polite clerk at the reception desk at your hotel assures you that a letter you've been waiting for has not arrived. You want to respond politely. He says to you, "I'm sorry, Madame. Maybe your letter will be in the afternoon mail.")
>
> Question: Comment répondriez-vous poliment au commis? (How would you respond politely to the clerk?)[32]

This variation of the item involves production of language "delicacy." Howard admits that there may be difficulty in accounting properly for students' language level, personality, maturity, experience--"and even legitimate idiosyncrasies" (p. 279). She does not see this as a real problem if the test designer affords enough practice materials in similar situations prior to the test.

H. Dictation and Variations on Dictation (Reading/Listening/Writing)

Various opinions have been expressed about the value of dictation as an integrative skills test. Oller (1973) is perhaps the principal proponent of this type of test format, though many other educators have been supporting its use for years. One advantage of dictation is that it can combine many discrete points of grammar and vocabulary in natural language contexts, especially if all the dictated sentences follow one another logically to form a whole paragraph. Variations on dictation might include some of the ideas listed below.

- Dictation of questions in the target language. Students write target-language answers to questions that follow each other logically, or all questions relate to a single theme.
- Partial or "spot" dictations. Students fill in gaps on their written copy of a passage.
- Full dictation of passage.
- Dictation of sentences in random order, all of which, when rearranged, form a logical paragraph or conversation. Students write dictated material, then rearrange.
- Dictation of directions for arriving at a destination. Students follow the dictated directions on an accompanying map.
- Dictation of descriptive passage. Students choose appropriate picture matching description from several options.
- Dictation of passage. Students answer comprehension questions in the native language related to the dictated material. The questions are presented on their test papers below the space allocated for the passage.

All the variations on dictation suggested here require students to process for its content the language they have taken down verbatim. Scoring of these items may become complicated, however, as it is again important to avoid "double jeopardy" for items missed on both the dictation and on the follow-up task. These and other testing problems need to be addressed as new communicative and situationalized formats are developed in the future.

I. Translation and Translation Cues (Writing)

The translation task is still a viable option for tests of writing skills; though some foreign language educators are uncomfortable with the use of the native language that this entails, one can argue that translation--at least at the beginning levels--represents a major type of cognitive activity associated with language learning. Some of the advantages of translation include the need to recall appropriate structures and vocabulary and the need to join these individual elements of language into meaningful thoughts. Translation, therefore, involves both analysis and synthesis of language elements, and represents a cognitive task that should reap real benefits for language learners as they develop their competence in the new idiom.

Traditionally, translation tests have consisted of random lists of sentences to be rendered into the native or target language, although one occasionally runs across tests where whole paragraphs or intact passages are used. What is suggested here is that for testing written skills, translation tests be used in some contextualized way, and that the task require students to go from the native language into the target language exclusively.

In order to make translation serve communicative language goals, the text to be translated ought to be representative of communicative language use. One might be required to write a letter in the foreign language, for example, imagining that a friend wanted to write to a native speaker of that language and requested help.

An alternative to word-for-word translation is the translation cue. This following example was designed as a follow-up to a partial translation item in which a police inspector was investigating a murder at the LeRoux mansion outside of Paris. Some continuity between sections of the test is therefore provided. Students are given a set of indirect questions that they must transform to direct questions, or they must change indirect discourse to direct discourse, as in the sample item below.

Sample 1.

> You are helping the chief inspector of police, who is interviewing various guests at the LeRoux mansion outside of Paris on the night of the murder. Suppose you are asked to interview the butler. Formulate in French appropriate questions to find out the following information.
>
> Ask the butler:
> how long he has been working here.
> if he knows the guests personally.
> where he worked three years ago.
> what he was doing while the guests were playing cards.
> if he knows how the murder was committed.

The translation item is integrative in the sense that many elements of the foreign language are synthesized to complete the task. It is also diagnostic and enables the teacher to pinpoint those structures and vocabulary items that students have not yet mastered. When done well, translation tasks can be "seeded" with many discrete points of grammar and lexicon and represent an efficient way to test a variety of points in context.

The previous item can be used to test question formation, as well as other specific points of grammar, by using indirect discourse cues in the target language instead of in the native language. This variation changes the nature of the task: the need to recall vocabulary and structures in the foreign language is eliminated to some extent; however, it does still constitute a mixed-skills item, combining reading comprehension with written production, as in the German version below:

Sample 2.

Sie helfen dem Polizisten, der an die verschiedenen Gästen von dem Haus Schmidt außerhalb Köln, während der Nacht des Mordes, Fragen stellt. Stellen Sie sich vor, daß Sie den Butler interviewen. Stellen Sie gute deutsche Fragen, um die folgenden Auskünfte zu erfahren.

Fragen Sie den Butler:
wie lange er hier schon arbeitet.
ob er die Gäste persönlich kennt.
wo er vor drei Jahren gearbeitet hat.
ob er weiß, wie der Mord begangen wurde.

(You are helping the policeman who is interviewing the guests at the Schmidt house outside of Köln, on the night of the murder. Imagine that you are interviewing the butler. Ask the correct German questions to find out the following information.

Ask the butler:
how long he has been working here.
if he knows the guests personally.
where he worked three years ago.
if he knows how the murder was committed.)

Again, this task, as well as other mixed-skills items discussed in this section, is integrative in nature; because this is so, failure to answer appropriately may be due to one or more of the following problems:

- Failure to comprehend the situational (German) paragraph introducing the indirect question cues

- Failure to comprehend the German indirect question cues themselves

- Failure to transform the indirect question cues to direct questions, either because of a lack of requisite grammatical knowledge or because of a misunderstanding of the task itself and what it entails

The first of these problems may really have little effect on the eventual answer produced by the students, especially if they understand the indirect question cues. The last problem mentioned--misunderstanding of the task itself--can be avoided if students have enough prior practice in switching from indirect discourse to direct discourse in class. Many teachers find, however, that students often react with some confusion to indirect questions: when given the stimulus "Demandez à X s'il a un frère," many students invariably will respond, "S'il a un frère." They seem to have fewer problems if the indirect question is in the native language. When cued "Ask X if he has a brother," most students understand that they are to formulate the question "X, do you have a brother?" Failure to produce the question is usually due to a lack of vocabulary or grammatical knowledge. For this reason, it is perhaps preferable to use translation cues on tests rather than target-language indirect question cues, although some teachers may prefer the latter because of a distaste for translation.

J. Strategic Competence in Writing: Some Possible Formats

As mentioned earlier, strategic competence is one aspect of communicative ability that may be extremely helpful to beginning language learners, since it involves the ability to use nonverbal and verbal communication strategies to compensate for breakdowns in communication, due to interference, distraction, or insufficient knowledge. Some of these strategies can be developed via classroom activities and tested on unit exams and quizzes. Classroom tasks that will help develop some of these strategies include (1) thinking of paraphrases for unknown vocabulary or expressions; (2) thinking of synonyms; (3) asking additional questions for needed information; and (4) guessing at unknown words in listening or reading materials. The last-named skill can be developed via cloze-type tasks such as those discussed under reading comprehension formats. The first three skills may be developed through speaking and writing practice activities and tested in both oral and written exams.

Sample 1.

Paraphrasing. Imagine you are describing your house or apartment in the U.S. to a French friend, but that you can't recall the names of the following objects, rooms of the house, etc. How can you get across your meaning without using the words themselves? Think of a definition, description, or short paraphrase for each of the following words, using the model as your guide.

Modèle: (dining room) "C'est la pièce où il y a une table pour manger." ("It's the room where there's a table for eating.")

a) the bathroom
b) the bureau (in the bedroom)
c) the curtains
d) the back yard

Sample 2.

Synonyms. Racontez l'histoire suivante. Remplacez l'expression soulignée par un verbe pronominal (reflexive).

A sept heures du matin, Sylvie ouvre les yeux, elle sort de son lit, fait sa toilette, et met ses vêtements. A huit heures, elle quitte la maison. Au travail, elle commence à parler au téléphone. Sylvie finit de travailler vers six heures; elle fait une promenade et parfois ses amies et elle vont nager à la piscine. Le soir, elle va au lit et elle trouve le sommeil très vite.

(Synonyms. Tell the following story. Replace the underlined expression with a reflexive verb.

At seven a.m., Sylvie opens her eyes, she gets out of the bed, washes up, and puts on her clothes. At eight o'clock, she leaves the house. At work, she starts to talk on the phone. Sylvie finishes working about six o'clock; she takes a walk and sometimes her friends and she go swimming at the pool. In the evening, she goes to bed and she falls asleep very quickly.)[33]

(In French, all the underlined verbs have reflexive counterparts.)

In both items above, students learn that there is more than one way to express one's meaning in the foreign language, and develop some confidence in their own communicative strategies. Such tasks encourage creativity and flexibility--important skills in developing strategic competence in another language.

K. "Open-Ended" Personalized Questions

Another type of writing item that allows for divergent answers, while still focusing on the vocabulary and structures to some extent, is the personalized question. Such questions can be used on quizzes, unit tests, and general achievement tests; the questions themselves might be oral or written, dictated to students or presented on the test paper. On the exam in which these questions appeared (see Appendix A), students were given a choice: they were told to answer eight questions out of the eleven given, using two- to three-sentence answers. Equal credit was awarded for both comprehensibility of the answer (content) and accuracy (grammatical correctness).

Sample 1.

Choisissez huit (8) questions et répondez à ces questions avec deux ou trois phrases complètes.

a) Où habitez-vous à l'université? Décrivez votre chambre.
b) Qu'est-ce que vous étudiez à l'université? Combien de cours avez-vous? Quels sont les jours où vous allez à ces cours et à quelle heure allez-vous en cours?
c) Comment trouvez-vous la vie universitaire?
d) Quel est votre repas préféré et qu'est-ce que vous mangez et buvez?...

(Choose eight questions and respond with two- to three-sentence answers.

a) Where do you live at the university? Describe your room.
b) What are you studying at the university? How many courses do you have? What days do you go to these courses and at what time?
c) What do you think of university life?
d) What is your favorite meal and what do you eat and drink?...)

A choice in answering questions is given so that students who may experience a "mental block" on one particular item are able to demonstrate their skills in another domain. Some students may also have very little to say about a certain topic, either in the second language or in the native language, but can think of much more to discuss about another topic. Because the questions are open-ended and not focused on particular vocabulary or grammar, each question can be scored for its comprehensibility, appropriateness, content, and accuracy.

IV. ORAL SKILLS FORMATS

One of the most difficult types of tests to create, schedule, administer, and grade is the oral test. Suggestions for oral testing, along with descriptions of possible scoring procedures, have been discussed in many sources, including Bartz (1979), Howard (1980), Linder (1977), Schulz and Bartz (1975), Valette (1977), and Valdman (1981). One of the professional priorities in classroom testing for the 1980s is the development of good tests of oral proficiency that can measure global communicative skills while enabling teachers to gather diagnostic information at the same time. Nowhere else in our classroom testing programs can we get across to students the message that communicative language use is a major goal of instruction.

A. Taped Exams

Oral tests can vary from those in which students respond in a laboratory to tape-recorded materials to those in which face-to-face oral interviews, such as the ACTFL/ETS oral proficiency interview, are used. Valdman (1981) describes a taped oral exam developed at Indiana University for first-semester French students. The Indiana University French Communicative Ability Test (IUFCAT) consists of three sections: Part I, pictorially cued responses; Part II, personal questions; and Part III, situational responses.[34]

Valdman's test uses three scoring criteria: (1) semantic and pragmatic appropriateness, (2) grammaticality and correct form of lexical items, and (3) fluency and accuracy, with greater weight given to the first two categories. Although answers are somewhat open-ended on some parts of the IUFCAT as described, the nature of the exam seems less integrative and less interactive than some of the other options available for achievement testing of oral skills.

B. Monologues and Exchanges

Several ideas for oral test formats have been proposed by Boylan (1982), who has developed a series of oral tests in Spanish for beginning and intermediate students at the University of Illinois. Such tests might be given during a course of study, with a more general oral proficiency interview administered as a final exam. In the fourth-semester Spanish course, for example, students take an oral test in which they engage in both monologues and conversational exchanges. Students randomly draw two or three topics from a set of topic cards (related to topics discussed in class). Each topic card has a set of opinion questions as a guide for the monologue portion of the exam. After the students give their impromptu monologue on one of the topics chosen, the instructor asks follow-up questions based on the information they have provided. A second part of the oral test consists of an interview in which students pose questions for the instructor, based either on one of the other topic cards chosen initially or on a role-play situation. Two sample topic cards given to the student for the monologue portion of the interview are provided below:

Sample 1.

"Los peligros y beneficios de la tecnología" ("The Dangers and Benefits of Technology"). You may wish to include the following in your monologue:

- Some benefits that we have received from modern technological discoveries and inventions
- Some of the negative effects that modern technology may create/has created
- What the government's role should be with respect to technology and industrialization

Sample 2.

"Los métodos de comunicación: la televisión y la prensa" ("Methods of Communication: Television and the Press"). You may wish to include the following in your monologue:

- As forms of communication, what are the advantages/disadvantages of television and newspapers?
- What, if any, are the various effects of television on children?
- Should TV and the press always reflect reality?
- What are your feelings with regard to advertising in newspapers and on TV?

Boylan provides teaching assistants with a set of questions they may want to use in the interview following the monologue. Teaching assistants may ask other questions as well, but the questions provided serve as both a guide and a reliability control measure so that test questions asked during interviews are consistent from one student to the next. The following questions are to be used with the monologue topics described above:

"Los peligros y beneficios de la tecnología"

a) ¿Cuál es un aparato tecnológico que usas frecuentemente?

¿Si no existiera este aparato, de qué manera sería diferente tu vida?

b) ¿Piensas que las máquinas tienen demasiado control en nuestra vida? ¿por qué sí/por qué no? Da ejemplos.
c) ¿Estarías mas contento si vivieras en un país menos tecnológico? ¿por qué sí/por qué no?
d) ¿Apoyas el uso/desarrollo de la energía atómica? ¿por qué sí/por qué no?

"Los métodos de comunicación: la televisión y la prensa"

a) ¿Cuáles son algunos efectos negativos que la televisión puede causar en los adultos?
b) ¿Cuál es tu programa favorito? ¿por qué te gusta?
c) Si tuvieras hijos, ¿cómo controlarías los programas que miraran en la televisión?
d) Si no existiera la televisión, ¿de qué manera sería diferente la vida del norteamericano promedio?
e) ¿Piensas que deben existir límites en la libertad de la prensa? ¿en qué casos?
f) ¿Debe la prensa expresar opiniones, o sólo debe reportar las noticias? Explica.
g) ¿Cuáles son algunas diferencias entre los periódicos españoles y los norteamericanos? ¿Cuáles son algunas semejanzas entre ellos?

("The Dangers and Benefits of Technology")

a) What is a technological device that you use frequently? If this device didn't exist, how would your life be different?
b) Do you think machines have too much control of our lives? Why or why not? Give examples.
c) Would you be happier if you lived in a country that was less technologically oriented? Why or why not?
d) Do you support the use/development of atomic energy? Why or why not?

"Methods of Communication: Television and the Press"

a) What are some negative effects that television can cause among adults?
b) What is your favorite program? Why do you like it?
c) If you had children, how would you control the programs they watch on television?
d) If television didn't exist, how would the middle-class North American person's life be different?
e) Do you think there ought to be limitations on the freedom of the press? In what situations?
f) Should the press express opinions, or just report facts? Explain.

g) What are some differences between Spanish and North American periodicals? What are some of the similarities between them?)

In the third section of the exam, Boylan provides students with English cues on interview cards for each topic. An example for the topic on advantages and disadvantages of technology is given below:

"Los peligros y benefícios de la tecnologí́a." For those who did Arreola's story, you might like this one:

Your instructor is a door-to-door salesperson, trying to sell the revolutionary new household product, "Plastitex." He or she has already described the product to you, but you want to obtain some more information before making a decision. You may want to find out the following:

- How much the product costs
- If it has a guarantee
- If it could cause any dangerous effects
- How long the product has been on the market
- How it was tested before going on sale
- If he or she has sold many in your neighborhood

In Figure 3, the instrument used by Boylan to rate student performance on oral exams is provided.

Fig. 3. Rating instrument.

SPANISH 124 ORAL FINAL EXAM STUDENT__________

Part I: Monologue (34%)

Fluency	1 2 3 4 5 6	______
Vocabulary	1 2 3 4 5 6 7 8	______
Structure	1 2 3 4 5 6	______
Comprehensibility	1 2 3 4 5 6 7 8 9 10 11 12 13 14	______
	Section total	______/34

Part II: Answering Questions on Monologue (26%)

Fluency	1 2 3 4 5	______
Vocabulary	1 2 3	______
Structure	1 2 3 4	______
Comprehensibility	1 2 3 4 5 6 7 8	______
Listening Comp.	1 2 3 4 5 6	______
	Section total	______/26

Fig. 3. (continued)

Part III: Interview (Asking Questions) (40%)

Fluency	1 2 3 4 5 6	
Vocabulary	1 2 3 4 5 6 7 8	________
Structure	1 2 3 4 5 6	________
Comprehensibility	1 2 3 4 5 6 7 8 9 10 11 12	________
Listening Comp.	1 2 3 4 5 6 7 8	________
		________
	Section total	/40
	Test total	/100

Weighting of Scales

Vocabulary--19%
Fluency--17%
Structure--16%
Comprehensibility--34%
Listening Comprehension--14%

DEFINITIONS FOR SCALE INTERVALS

Part I: Monologue (34%)

Fluency

1 Speech halting and fragmentary; long, unnatural pauses, or utterances left unfinished

2 Speech very slow and uneven except for short or routine sentences

3 Speech frequently hesitant and jerky; sentences may be left uncompleted

4 Some definite stumbling, but manages to rephrase or continue

5 Speech generally natural and continuous; only slight stumbling or unnatural pauses

6 Speech natural and continuous; no unnatural pauses

Vocabulary (breadth and precision of usage)

1-2 Lacks basic words; inadequate; inaccurate usage
3-4 Often lacks needed words; somewhat inaccurate usage
5-6 Occasionally lacks basic words; generally accurate usage
7-8 Rich and extensive vocabulary; very accurate usage

Structure

1 No utterances structurally correct

2 Very few utterances structurally correct

Fig. 3. (continued)

3	Some utterances rendered correctly, but major structural problems remain
4	Many correct utterances, but with definite structural problems
5	Most utterances rendered correctly, with some minor structural errors
6	Utterances almost always correct

<u>Comprehensibility</u>

1-3	Almost entirely/entirely incomprehensible to native speaker of Spanish
4-6	Mostly incomprehensible; occasional phrases comprehensible
7-9	Many errors, about half incomprehensible
10-12	Many errors, but still mostly comprehensible
13-14	Almost entirely/entirely comprehensible to native speaker of Spanish; only an occasional word not comprehensible/no words incomprehensible

<u>Part II: Answering Questions on Monologue (26%)</u>

<u>Fluency</u>

1	Speech halting and fragmentary; long, unnatural pauses or utterances
2	Speech frequently hesitant and jerky; sentences may be left uncompleted
3	Some definite stumbling, but manages to rephrase or continue
4	Speech generally natural and continuous; only slight stumbling or unnatural pauses
5	Speech natural and continuous; no unnatural pauses

<u>Vocabulary</u> (breadth and precision of usage)

1	Lacks basic words; inadequate; inaccurate usage
2	Occasionally lacks basic words; generally accurate usage
3	Extensive vocabulary; accurate usage

<u>Structure</u>

1	Few/no utterances structurally correct
2	Some utterances correct, but major structural problems remain

Fig. 3. (continued)

3 Many correct utterances, but definite structural problems remain

4 Utterances almost always correct

Comprehensibility

1-2 Incomprehensible/almost incomprehensible to native speaker of Spanish

3-4 Many errors that impede comprehensibility, less than half understandable

5-6 Some/few errors, but still mostly comprehensible

7-8 Almost or totally comprehensible to native speaker of Spanish

Listening Comprehension

1-2 Student comprehends nothing/little of what instructor says

3-4 Student comprehends some/a lot of what instructor says

5-6 Student comprehends most/all of what instructor says

Part III: Interview (Asking Questions) (40%)

Fluency

1 Speech halting and fragmentary; long, unnatural pauses or utterances

2 Speech very slow and uneven, except for short or routine sentences

3 Speech frequently hesitant and jerky; sentences may be left uncompleted

4 Some definite stumbling, but manages to rephrase or continue

5 Speech generally natural and continuous; only slight stumbling or unnatural pauses

6 Speech natural and continuous; no unnatural pauses

Vocabulary (breadth and precision of usage)

1-2 Lacks basic words; inadequate, inaccurate usage
3-4 Often lacks needed words; somewhat inaccurate usage
5-6 Occasionally lacks basic words; generally accurate usage
7-8 Rich and extensive vocabulary; very accurate usage

Fig. 3. (continued)

Structure

1	No utterances rendered correctly
2	Very few utterances rendered correctly
3	Some utterances rendered correctly, but major structural problems remain
4	Many correct utterances, but with definite structural problems
5	Most utterances rendered correctly, with some minor structural errors
6	Utterances almost always correct

Comprehensibility

1-2	Entirely/almost entirely incomprehensible to native speaker of Spanish
3-4	Mostly incomprehensible; occasional phrases comprehensible
5-6	Many errors, about half incomprehensible
7-8	Many errors, but still mostly comprehensible
9-10	Almost entirely comprehensible to native speaker of Spanish; only an occasional word not comprehensible
11-12	Entirely comprehensible to native speaker of Spanish; no words incomprehensible

Listening Comprehension

2	Student comprehends one instructor answer
4	Student comprehends two instructor answers
6	Student comprehends three instructor answers
8	Student comprehends four instructor answers

C. Interviews

The oral interview test described below is administered following the first eight weeks of the first-semester (French 101) course at the University of Illinois. (The final exam for oral skills is much like the oral proficiency interview developed for academic situations by ACTFL/ETS.) The midsemester test consists of a set of conversation cards that serve as a focal point for the oral interview. Students may be interviewed individually or in pairs, depending upon (1) time constraints, (2) the desire to provide native or near-native input to the interview (when done with one student) versus the desire to provide students with the security and comfort of working with a partner during the exam, and (3) the teacher's individual preference for a one-on-one interview format versus a format in which he or she can be observer and notetaker without active participation. Individual instructors should choose a format that meets their own needs as well as those of their students, but the sample test provided here will serve just as well for individual and paired interviews.

Individual Interviews

The teacher sets up a 15-20 minute appointment with each student in the class for the oral test. To begin the interview, both the teacher and the student select at random from a set of conversation cards one card that will serve as a focal point for the interview.

Sample 1.

SITUATION B, CARD (1).

Vous parlez de votre chambre à l'université. Posez les questions suivantes. Posez d'autres questions aussi, avec des mots comme "comment," "combien," "pourquoi," "quand."

(You're talking about your room at the university. Ask the following questions. Ask other questions, too, using words like "how," "how much," "why," "where," "when.")

Ask your partner:
- how he is today.
- whom he lives with at the university.
- if there is a telephone in his room.
- if his friends like to visit his room.
- how old his roommate is.

SITUATION B, CARD (2).

Vous êtes propriétaire et vous avez une chambre d'étudiant à louer. Vous parlez à un(e) étudiant(e). Posez les questions suivantes. Posez d'autres questions aussi, avec des mots comme "comment," "combien," "pourquoi," "où," "quand."

(You're a landlord and you have a student's room for rent. You're speaking to a student. Ask the following questions. Ask other questions, too, using words like "how," "how much," "why," "where," "when.")

Ask your partner:
- how he is today.
- where he is a student.

if he has any animals.
if he has a television, radio, or stereo.
if he is a good, serious student.

The teacher begins the interview by using the conversation card he or she has chosen as a guide for interviewing the student. If a tape recorder is available, the teacher may want to tape the interview so that it can be played back when assigning a grade. Students might be asked to provide their own tapes, and can be allowed to keep them after the test to have a record of their own oral skills against which they can compare later speech samples. Some students may want to use the same tape to record the next oral exams, thus documenting their own progress throughout their coursework in the foreign language on a single tape or set of tapes. This allows them to see dramatically the progress they have made, which motivates them to continue with further study. Another option is for the teacher to take down on the left side of the score sheet the student's responses in the first portion of the interview (see Figure 4), making notes as to strong and weak points in the student's speech.

When the instructor has finished his or her portion of the interview, the student asks the questions on the conversation card and the instructor answers. Again, the teacher takes notes of the student's performance. It is best to take down exactly what the student says so that the speech sample is accurately represented. Later, grades will be assigned on the basis of that speech sample, so it is important during the interview to make notes of pronunciation and fluency as well.

The conversation cards should serve as a stimulus for conversation and should not be used as a translation task exclusively. Teachers should feel free to expand the interview, taking care not to push the students beyond their current level of linguistic competence, or at least to limit additional questions to those that they could reasonably be expected to answer at this point in their instruction. Students should also be encouraged to expand the interview by asking follow-up questions for any answers the instructor gives; note that directions for this type of expansion are given on the conversation cards themselves.

Paired Interviews

In this variant of the oral interview test, the teacher sets up a 30-minute session for each pair of students. Each student chooses a conversation card to begin the exam. One student asks the questions first, while the other responds. In the second part of the exam, the roles are reversed. The instructor does not enter into the interview process directly unless one of the students is having difficulty communicating with the other;

otherwise, the instructor takes notes on the speech of both students during the course of their conversation. It might be best to use the left side of the score sheet (Figure 4) for Student A and the right side for Student B. As in the individual interview, notes should be taken on pronunciation and fluency as well as on the actual sentence elements produced, and students should be encouraged to expand the interview by using follow-up questions.

Scoring the Interview Test

On the basis of the speech protocol of each student, the instructor assigns a grade of A through E for each of four categories: pronunciation, vocabulary, grammar, and fluency. A conversion table is provided at the bottom of the sheet, allowing for some variability in the letter grade categories. For example, a very good performance might be given an A or 5.0 grade, whereas a slightly poorer performance, though still meriting an A, may be given an A-, or 4.5 grade. The instructor can check one box in each category and then convert each letter grade assigned this way into a number. The number obtained is entered in the first space to the right of the box and multiplied by the weight provided: pronunciation 4; vocabulary 7; grammaticality 6; and fluency 3. The sum of the weighted scores will add up to 100 if all categories receive a grade of 5 (A).

The weighting of pronunciation, vocabulary, grammar, and fluency has been determined on the basis of research using the FSI Oral Proficiency Interview, which shows that learners in the 0-1+ range (beginning competence) have speech profiles that reflect primarily their knowledge of vocabulary and least their fluency and sociolinguistic competence (Higgs and Clifford 1981). For more advanced students, the weights for the oral interview would be adjusted somewhat differently, i.e., more weight might be assigned to grammatical accuracy and fluency in intermediate courses, where these are the goals being emphasized; sociolinguistic accuracy and appropriateness might be weighted more heavily in advanced courses.

At the end of each semester in French 101 through 104 at the University of Illinois, an oral proficiency interview is scheduled for each student. The interview procedure used is the ACTFL/ETS oral interview, in which a 15- to 20-minute conversation is held with the student, who is then rated using the scales given in Appendix B. At the novice and intermediate-low ranges, this interview will resemble a general achievement test, due to the limited nature of the students' skills and knowledge of the language at that level. At higher levels of proficiency, material not specifically dealt with in the course *per se* might nevertheless be explored in the effort to probe students to the limit of their abilities and elicit a ratable sample that provides an indication of the best that they can do. Preliminary

Fig. 4. Score sheet for oral tests.

FRENCH 101 & 102 SPEAKING TEST: STUDENT SCORE SHEET

Name ______________________

NOTES:

Pronunciation

E	D	C	B	A

__ x4 = __

Vocabulary

E	D	C	B	A

__ x7 = __

Grammar

E	D	C	B	A

__ x6 = __

Fluency

E	D	C	B	A

__ x3 = __

Total = __

A = 4.5 - 5.0
B = 4.0 - 4.4
C = 3.5 - 3.9
D = 3.0 - 3.4
E = 2.0 - 2.9

Name ______________________

NOTES:

Pronunciation

E	D	C	B	A

__ x4 = __

Vocabulary

E	D	C	B	A

__ x7 = __

Grammar

E	D	C	B	A

__ x6 = __

Fluency

E	D	C	B	A

__ x3 = __

Total = __

A = 4.5 - 5.0
B = 4.0 - 4.4
C = 3.5 - 3.9
D = 3.0 - 3.4
E = 2.0 - 2.9

results of oral interviews in our first- and second-year language courses have indicated that students fall within the range of novice to advanced (ILR 0 through 2), with many of the students in the first year in the intermediate ranges and quite a few close to or in the advanced range in the second year. (Grades for these tests are assigned using the same score sheet described earlier and illustrated in Figure 4.)

In the second-semester course at the University of Illinois, French students go to a "survival lab" held during the middle of the semester for a two-week period. A classroom or lounge area is reserved for 40 hours (20 hours per week) where French 102 students can have a "live encounter" with native or near-native speakers in role-plays of survival situations that are drawn from the ACTFL/ETS interview procedure. (See Liskin-Gasparro, 1981, for examples of these situations.) The survival lab is staffed by teaching assistants and professors, and students are required to work successfully through two role-plays randomly chosen from a set of role-play cards, in order to "pass" this portion of the course requirements. Students who are unsuccessful can return to the lab at another time and try again.

Because survival situations are used in every intermediate-level oral proficiency interview, the survival lab serves to verify that students in the second-semester course are capable of handling themselves at least at the intermediate-low level and can accomplish such tasks as finding a hotel room, getting food in a restaurant, getting gas at a station, having a medical problem taken care of, and the like. During the first semester that the survival lab was instituted, French 102 students responded extremely favorably to this midterm test, and many said that they felt gratified that they were already able to function so well in the target language after one and one-half semesters of work. Most students were especially pleased that the survival lab allowed them the opportunity to try out their oral skills in real-world survival situations, especially with people they had not met before.

In order to prepare students for both the survival lab and the oral proficiency interview, we have developed a series of videotaped role-play situations in which native speakers either interact with one another or with an American in a variety of encounters that foreigners might have in the target culture. Print materials accompany each of the tapes so that students can follow up the viewing of the role-play with classroom activities designed to help them deal with similar situations. Other ideas for classroom activities are discussed in the next section.

D. Preparing Students for Oral Tests: Some Classroom Activities

In order to afford abundant practice in both listening and speaking for as many students as possible during the class hour, activities like those on the oral tests just described should be done in class in pairs or in small groups. All these activities can be used as a substitute for manipulative drills, as long as the teacher is careful to analyze the task demands of a given activity and match the outcomes with the practice afforded by a less interesting sequence of drill material. For example, if a sequence of five-minute drills in the text will enable students to practice the formation of the past tense of certain verbs, a well-chosen conversation card or interview card can be designed to accomplish that same end in a more interesting (and more communicative) fashion, using an equivalent amount of class time.

Each of the pair or group activities suggested below operates on the assumption that everyone involved has some unique information to contribute to the others in the group. In other words, an "information gap" exists within every group of students, and only when all students listen actively to what everyone else has to say will that information gap be filled.

Conversation Cards

Students are grouped in threes for these activities. Each student receives a card on which question prods are given. Two students are given translation cues in their native language, while the third student serves as the group "checker" (the "checker" has the correct form of the questions that the other two students have to ask and is responsible for correcting them). Questions are personalized, providing for divergent answers. Again, students in the group are encouraged to ask follow-up questions to keep the conversation going. If students have difficulty or are not sure about the accuracy of their answers, they can summon the teacher for individual help. After students have completed the interview, the teacher may ask each group to "report back" any interesting information obtained during the activity, either orally or in writing. Some sample conversation cards are provided below.

CARTE DE CONVERSATION

1) Ask your partner:
    how old he/she is.
    where he/she is from.
    if he/she likes the University of Illinois.
        why or why not?
    how many courses he/she has this semester.

2) Ask your partner:
    why he/she is studying French.
    when he/she works the most. (le plus)
    where he/she wants to live later. (plus tard)
    if he/she has a cat/dog. How many? Why?

3) Correcteur/Correctrice

Carte (1)
Quel âge as-tu? (Quel âge est-ce que tu as?)
D'où es-tu? (D'où viens-tu?)
Est-ce que tu aimes l'Université d'Illinois?
Pourquoi/pourquoi pas?
Combien de cours est-ce que tu as ce semestre?

Carte (2)
Pourquoi est-ce que tu étudies le français?
Quand est-ce que tu travailles le plus?
Où est-ce que tu as envie d'habiter plus tard?
Est-ce que tu as un chien/chat? Combien? Pourquoi?[35]

Interviews

A different type of interview sheet is illustrated below. Each student receives the sheet and uses it to interview someone else. Then in groups of three to five, students do the "brainstorm" activities and report back their results to the whole class.

DESCRIPTIVE ADJECTIVES -- DESCRIBING YOURSELF OR SOMEONE YOU KNOW

INTERVIEW: Ask your partner some of the following questions to find out about his/her personality. Your partner can qualify his or her answer by using an adverb like "toujours," "parfois," "souvent," or "jamais."

Etes-vous...

agréable ou désagréable?
altruiste ou égoïste?
artiste ou sans talent (without talent)
bizarre ou normal?
calme ou agité?
conformiste ou nonconformiste?
raisonnable ou déraisonnable?
décontracté (relaxed) ou nerveux(-se)?
difficile ou agréable?
drôle ou sérieux(-se)?

énergique ou apathique?
excentrique ou ordinaire?
hypocrite ou honnête?
idéaliste ou réaliste?
impatient ou patient?
individualiste ou conformiste?
intelligent ou bête?
insociable ou sociable?
optimiste ou pessimiste?
simple ou compliqué?
snob ou sympathique?

GROUP BRAINSTORM: In your groups think of as many people fitting the following descriptions as you can. Say the first person who comes to mind.

Nommez une personne...
drôle
sincère
excentrique
snob
individualiste
idéaliste

GROUP BRAINSTORM: Think of as many adjectives as you can to describe the following people.

la femme idéale:
un homme typique:
Julia Child:
Ronald Reagan:
Ralph Nader:
Farrah Fawcett:
le (la) camarade de chambre idéal(e):
le patron (la patronne) (boss) idéal(e):
le professeur idéal:
l'étudiant idéal:
le chauffeur de taxi idéal:
le dentiste idéal:
(?)

Incomplete Maps

Map activities can be designed in which parts of the map are missing (the "information gap"). Students are placed in groups of three, each with a copy of the map. The teacher distributes information cards to each of the students. By sharing this "secret" information, students in the group fill in the missing portions of the town. (See Omaggio 1982 for sample materials for this and other interactive activities.)

Debates

At intermediate and advanced levels, students might like to try debating certain issues or topics in groups of two or more. The activity sheet includes functional vocabulary for expressing one's opinion and taking a position. Students choose one of the topics given at the top of the sheet and try to incorporate the functional vocabulary during the course of their remarks.

SUJETS DE DEBAT

Quelles sont vos opinions sur les questions suivantes? Etes-vous pour ou contre?

- Les expériences nucléaires sont nécessaires pour le progrès.

- Les drogues (comme l'alcool et le marijuana) sont nuisibles (harmful) à la société et doivent être interdites.

- Une société sans classe ne pourra jamais exister dans un système capitaliste.

- Il faut supprimer la vente des armements aux régimes de droite en Amérique du Sud.

COMMENT PRENDRE POSITION: MOTS UTILES POUR VOUS EXPRIMER

Je ne suis pas d'accord avec vous.
Pardon, mais....
Vous avez tort/raison.
Ne savez-vous pas que....
Supposons que....
Voilà mon hypothèse....
J'en conclus que....
Cette proposition n'est pas pratique/réalisable.
C'est une impossibilité/une contradiction.
A mon avis....
Pour ma part....

Selon moi....
Mon point de vue est le suivant:
Personnellement, je suis pour/contre....
Je considère que....
Vous avez des préjugés.
Il me semble que....
J'estime que....
Je suis convaincu/persuadé que....
Il est préférable de....

(*SUBJECTS FOR DEBATE*

What are your opinions on the following issues? Are you for or against them?

- Nuclear experimentation is necessary for progress.
- Drugs (like alcohol and marijuana) are harmful to society and should be forbidden.
- A classless society could never exist in a capitalistic system.
- We have to eliminate the sale of arms to right-wing régimes in South America.

HOW TO TAKE A POSITION: USEFUL WORDS FOR EXPRESSING YOURSELF[36]

I don't agree with you.
Excuse me, but....

You're wrong/right.
Don't you know that....
Let's suppose that....
Here's my theory:
I conclude from that that....
That idea isn't practical/possible.
That's an impossibility/a contradiction.
In my opinion....

According to me....
My point of view is the following:
Personally, I'm for/against....
I think that....
You have some preconceived notions.
It seems to me that....
I figure that....
I'm convinced/persuaded that....
It's preferable that....)

V. GUIDELINES FOR CREATING CONTEXTUALIZED TESTS

Many teachers may agree that it would be good to construct contextualized tests for their language classes, but believe that they simply do not have the time or the expertise to do so on a regular basis. Although creating contextualized tests may seem at first glance to be a much more difficult process than creating conventional exams, teachers will find that the process becomes much easier with practice. Because the contextualized test integrates many linguistic and lexical features in a few well-chosen contexts, the creation of the test is actually simpler than when the instrument consists of many unrelated items. Our experience at the University of Illinois has shown that (1) teaching assistants in French have learned within a short period of time to write good test items on the models given in the preceding pages; and (2) no one who has helped in the creation of contextualized tests wants to return to conventional testing methods. Students have also reported that they like these tests better than those they have had in previous courses; they find them more "interesting" and have felt challenged to use their "real" language skills when taking the exams.

A few guidelines are presented below for the teacher who would like to try to design test items of the type discussed in this book. If these steps are followed, preparation of quizzes and exams should be facilitated, and test construction will not take an inordinate amount of time. (It may be best to begin by trying to create a quiz or short unit exam rather than a long test.)

Step A. Take an inventory of the material to be covered on the test or quiz planned for the unit or lesson. List the major grammatical features, new vocabulary, and cultural content that you would like to elicit on the test.

Step B. Decide which skill areas you would like to emphasize on this test or quiz, and choose some formats from among the samples given in the preceding pages.

Step C. Divide the grammatical, lexical, and cultural content listed in step (A) among the item types chosen. Be sure to place appropriate emphasis on each aspect of the language you wish to test across skill areas. To do this, constructing a testing grid, such as the one in Figure 5, may be helpful.

Step D. Create a simple story, dialogue, or paragraph that includes the features you've identified for each part of the test. You may find that you can create your own context quite easily, especially if you keep the themes and cultural content of the lesson or unit in mind. For inspiration, you might want to look at reading passages, cultural commentary, or dialogues in your text, or choose a passage from a supplementary reader at the same level of difficulty. Some teachers may want to use authentic materials and "edit" them, seeding the edited version where necessary to elicit or include some of the linguistic features to be tested.

Fig. 5. Testing grid.*

Grammar/Vocabulary to Be Sampled on Test II	Listening/ Writing	Reading/ Writing	Writing
Avoir and avoir expressions	X	X	
Faire and faire expressions	X		X
Interrogative words and expressions; word order	X	X	X
Regular -ir verbs			X
-er verbs with spelling changes	X		X
Adjective agreement and placement	X		X
Negative; use of de after pas			X
Possessive adjectives		X	X
Vocabulary for lodging	X		X
Descriptive adjectives	X		X
Family vocabulary	X		X
Part of Test	I (Dictée with answers)	II (Question writing)	III (Room description) IV (Partial translation)
Point values:	15	25	60

*Used to create sample Unit Test II (French) in Appendix A

Step E. Figure out a scoring system that will assign points where you want them to be assigned; that is, give some points for accuracy, some for content, some for appropriate semantic choices, etc. Those features you want to stress should receive more total test points, and those that you consider of lesser importance should receive fewer points on the total test instrument.

Remember to consider including some global or divergent-production items on your test or quiz as well as the more discrete-point item types.

The steps outlined above were followed to create the tests included in Appendix A. Teaching assistants were involved in the preparation of each of the tests illustrated: in French, two assistants prepared the unit test with limited supervision; in Spanish, one teaching assistant created the test herself, following the same type of models as the ones in this paper. These instructors are novice teachers, but they have had very little difficulty learning how to create contextualized test items from the sample items given.

It is always a good idea to have a native speaker check the test you have created if you are not a native speaker yourself. If possible, try your test out on a colleague to see if there are any extraneous sources of difficulty or items that would not work well for some unanticipated reason.

Item Banks

Once the teacher has successfully created several versions of unit tests, quizzes, and semester exams for a given set of materials, it might be a good idea to begin an informal "item bank." Subsequent tests can then be generated by choosing whole items from the bank and combining them in a new way to create new versions of the original test. This is being done very successfully on a large scale in Ontario via the Ontario Assessment Instrument Pool for French as a Second Language (1980). The first 100 items, usable for proficiency and/or achievement testing purposes, have been field-tested and are available in a packet to teachers for a nominal fee. A second set of 100 items is being field-tested at this writing.

The test items in the bank are coded as to skill areas, type of competence, and grammatical content and are cross-referenced to a provincial curriculum guide developed a few years previously. It is hoped that this same type of coordination among proficiency guidelines, curriculum guides, and test items will be achieved in the United States. The process has already begun with the ACTFL Stepladder Project mentioned earlier. When these proficiency guidelines are in place, curriculum guides and test item banks should follow.

For teachers who would like to create their own item bank, Popyuk (1980) suggests a model that may be of use. His model is designed for second language proficiency testing, but there is no reason why it cannot also serve the needs of the classroom teacher for constructing achievement tests. Teachers might want to include the following information on a typical item-bank card:

- Unit test, quiz or semester exam on which the item has appeared
- Item format (i.e., skill area and nature of the task involved)
- Grammatical, lexical, sociolinguistic, or cultural feature(s) tested
- The test item itself (i.e., the cloze passage, partial translation, set of sentence cues, etc.)
- Item history (student performance data collected in terms of item difficulty in past exams); number of times (dates) item has been used previously

The possibilities for this type of test generation become more numerous as our technological capacities increase in the future, and it may be that item banks will be stored via computers accessible to many classroom teachers in the years to come.

VI. SUMMARY AND CONCLUSIONS

The suggestions for achievement testing presented in this paper are offered as a point of departure for further discussion as we search for viable ways to incorporate real language use into our day-to-day measurement of language competence. In the coming years, field-testing of these and similar formats will begin to yield validity and reliability data that will help us refine our testing materials. It is clear that the profession will have to devote a good deal more time and creative energy to the testing problem before we can make some significant changes that will affect instruction on a wide scale.

A list of professional priorities (see Omaggio 1981) for classroom testing should include:

- A national effort to develop operational definitions of proficiency in a foreign language, taking into account the real-world limitations inherent in learning a foreign language outside of the target culture (this is being done at this writing via the ACTFL Stepladder Project)
- The organization of follow-up conferences and workshops to devise model testing techniques that incorporate natural communicative language into tests of specific course-related goals, both linguistic and communicative
- The planning of regional and local inservice training workshops that would present these testing models to as large a number of classroom teachers as possible, and would help them develop measurement instruments to suit their own specific course materials
- Establishment of validity and reliability data via field-testing
- Development of item banks for widespread use
- Recommendations for the development of university-level courses in foreign language testing methods and the inclusion of such courses among the requirements for teacher certification
- Recommendations for continuing research studies relating to the testing techniques developed in the second item above to improve on the ideas as new knowledge is generated
- Recommendations to textbook publishers to include model foreign language tests with their packages of course materials

These recommendations parallel some of those made by Woodford (1980) in his recently published "plan for action" for foreign language testing. We cannot afford to continue to ignore the problems we have in this domain. The means by which we evaluate foreign language skills will determine, to a large extent, the success of foreign language programs in the future. These concerns should form the very core of our professional priorities in the 1980s.

APPENDIX A

Sample Unit Exams and Semester Exams

1. Spanish 101 Unit Exam
2. French 101 Unit Exam
3. French 101 Final Exam

SPANISH 101[37]

UNIT TEST II

CHAPTERS 3-5

Name ______________

Oral Communication ______

I. LISTENING COMPREHENSION

A. Dictation. You will hear two sentences read three times each. The first time, just listen; the second time, listen and write; the third time, listen for the complete message and make any necessary corrections. (7 points)

1. ______________________________
2. ______________________________

B. Paragraph Comprehension. Listen carefully to the following paragraph, which will be read twice only. Then answer the questions below in ENGLISH. (9 points)

1. What does Leonora want to do, and why?

____

2. What will she do there?

____

3. What does she plan to do soon?

____

C. Questions/Answers. Write a complete and logical answer in ENGLISH to the following questions. Write enough to indicate that you understand the question. A simple "yes" or "no" or the like will not be sufficient. Each question will be read twice. (6 points)

1. ______________________________
2. ______________________________

II. GRAMMAR/TRANSLATION

A. Verbs/Vocabulary. Fill in the blanks with the appropriate form of the given verb. Do not leave any answers blank as points are allocated for both vocabulary and the verb endings. (13.5 points)

Pedro and Leonora are entering the U of I's Study Abroad Program in Chile. Here they answer a barrage of questions from their parents.

1. (to begin) El programa __________ en dos semanas.

2. (to hope) Yo __________ aprender mucho.

3. (to understand) (not comprender) Tú __________ cuando hablo español, ¿no?

4. (to read) Nosotros __________ los libros sobre el país.

5. (to exist) Muchos problemas __________todavía.

6. (to want) (not desear) Pedro y yo no __________ estudiar todos los días.

B. Direct Object Pronouns

Next, Pedro and Leonora speak with a friend, who has a few questions. Answer the questions below, replacing all the direct objects with the appropriate direct object pronouns. (5 points)

Model: Do you have the plane tickets? Yes, we have them.

1. ¿Hablan Uds. español? Sí, ________________
2. ¿Comprenden Uds. las leyes del país? Sí, ________________
3. ¿Visitan Uds. la biblioteca? Sí, ________________
4. Leonora, ¿practicas muchos deportes? Sí, ________________
5. ¿Me llaman Uds. por teléfono? Sí, ________________

C. Cardinal Numbers.

As a final check for the departing students, a bit of arithmetic and destination description. Write out the following words and numbers: (5 points)

1. 34 + 53 = 87. ____________ + ____________ = ____________

2. 100 streets and 61 neighborhoods ________________________

D. Partial Translation.*

Leonora's first letter home is eagerly received and shows an interesting schedule of activities. Fill in the blanks with the Spanish equivalent of the words in parentheses. (30 points)

---

*See pp. 42-44 for alternate formats.

Queridos padres:

__________ apartamento está en _____________ cerca del océano.
(Our) (a building)

_______________, ___________________________ tomamos _______________
(On Saturdays) (if the weather is good) (the third bus)

a la playa. _____________ amigos _________________ pero yo siempre
(My) (fish)

________________. ___________ fin de semana, si _______________,
(have to study) (This) (it is cloudy)

_____________________ un concierto. ___________________________
(we are going to attend) (On Friday, December 1st)

cenamos con otros amigos en un restaurante que está en

___________________ del Hotel Buenavista. ________________________,
(the tenth floor) (On the 6th of January)

____________________ en Lugarbueno, porque allí ____________ muchas
(we have)

oportunidades interesantes.

____
(See you soon)

Leonora

E. Demonstrative Adjectives and Pronouns

Pedro has some free time for travel and visits Leonora. Here she gives him the grand tour. Write the form of the appropriate demonstrative adjective or pronoun in each blank. (11.5 points)

1. Las oficinas están en ___________ (those - far away) esquinas y los apartamentos están en ___________ (this one).

2. Los turistas visitan ___________ (that) museo, pero creo que ___________ (that one - far away) es muy interesante.

3. Muchas veces cenamos en ___________ (this) hotel pero a veces cenamos en ___________ (those).

4. ¡___________ (that) es estupendo!

F. Translation.

Back home once again, Leonora and Pedro treat their friends and families to slides and a detailed commentary. Translate the following into Spanish. Write out all numbers. (28 points)

1. From the church one must go by car six blocks to the post office.

____

____

2. At what time do they open the stores? They must open them at 4:00 P.M.

____

____

3. There are 41 islands in these lakes.

____

4. In the summer, everyone goes on vacation.

____

III. COMMUNICATION/COMPOSITION (15 points)

Pedro and Leonora's experience has convinced you. You decide to visit the heart of the Andes for yourself. When your parents hear this, they want some information, so you must write a letter answering some of the questions they have, such as the following:

- On what day and date does the program begin?
- How are you going to get there?
- At what time will you arrive in Chile?
- What will you do there?
- What do you have to take along?
- When will you return?

Write a minimum of 50 words in SPANISH, excluding proper nouns. Remember, you will be evaluated on the variety of your vocabulary and on grammatical accuracy and, most important, on your ability to convey a coherent message.

Queridos padres,

____

____

____

Con cariño,

IV. CULTURE. To be given by the instructor.

FRENCH 101

UNIT TEST II

INSTRUCTOR'S COPY

I. Dictée with answers. Read each question twice. Students are to take down the questions as a dictée, and then go back and answer them in complete sentences in French. (15 points; 3 points per question, 2 points per answer)

A. Préférez-vous un bel appartement moderne ou une petite maison?

B. Essayez-vous d'avoir toujours raison?

C. Faites-vous souvent la cuisine, ou mangez-vous au restaurant?

II. Une interview. A reporter for Paris Match is interviewing an American exchange student in Paris. You are transcribing the interview, but the reporter didn't tell you his questions! For each statement that Eddie makes, write an appropriate question in the blank provided. (25 points; 5 points each)

III. La chambre de Margot. Shown below is Margot's dormitory room. Using the vocabulary you know, answer the questions below the picture. (30 points; part I, 24 points, part II, 6 points)

IV. Une solution simple. Margot et Annick, sa camarade de chambre, détestent leur appartement. Un jour elles décident de chercher un autre logement. Complétez leur conversation. La conversation en anglais est à côté de la conversation en français. (30 points)

FRENCH 101
UNIT TEST II

NOM ________________

I. Dictée with Answers. Read each question twice. Students are to take down the questions as a dictée, and then go back and answer them in complete sentences in French. (15 points; 3 points per question, 2 points per answer)

A. ____
____

B. ____
____

C. ____
____

II. Une interview. A reporter for Paris Match is interviewing an American exchange student in Paris. You are transcribing the interview, but the reporter didn't tell you his questions! For each statement that Eddie makes, write an appropriate question in the blank provided. (25 points; 5 points each)

A. Le journaliste: ______________________________?
Eddie: Parce que j'ai envie d'étudier le français!

B. Le journaliste: ______________________________?
Eddie: J'ai vingt-quatre ans.

C. Le journaliste: ______________________________?
Eddie: Il y a quatre Américains dans ma classe ici.

D. Le journaliste: ______________________________?
Eddie: J'habite à Frederick, Maryland.

E. Le journaliste: ______________________________?
Eddie: Je rentre aux Etats-Unis le 12 avril.

III. La chambre de Margot. Shown below is Margot's dormitory room. Using the vocabulary you know, answer the questions below the picture. (30 points)

A. Describe Margot's room by completing the sentence below. Name eight objects in the room, and use a different adjective to describe each object. Choose the adjectives from the following list: ancien, beau, grand, joli, petit, noir, vert, vieux. Be sure to make the adjective agree and to place it appropriately. (24 points)

Dans la chambre de Margot, il y a __________, __________, __________, __________, __________, __________, __________, et __________.

B. Write two complete sentences in French telling what Margot does NOT have in her room. (6 points) ____________________
____

IV. <u>Une solution simple</u>. Margot et Annick, sa camarade de chambre, détestent leur appartement. Un jour elles décident de chercher un autre logement. Complétez leur conversation. La conversation en anglais est à côté de la conversation en français. (30 points)

Annick: Je n'aime pas _____ appartement. La cuisine est trop _____ et _____. En plus, c'est trop cher!	I don't like our apartment. The kitchen is too small, and there's no garden. Besides, it's too expensive!
Margot: _____ un appartement à louer près de l'université?	Doesn't your aunt have an apartment for rent near the university?
Annick: Ah oui! _____ _____! Je vais _____ téléphoner tout de suite!	Ah yes! That's true! I'm going to phone her right away!
AU TELEPHONE	ON THE PHONE
Annick: Allô, Patrick? Est-ce que _____ est là?...Oh, je vois, elle _____. Est-ce que nous pouvons voir _____ appartement dans la Rue Gervais cet après-midi? Nous _____trouver un _____appartement...Eh, bien, d'accord. A bientôt.	Hello, Patrick? Is your mother there?...Oh, I see. She's doing errands. Can we see her apartment on Gervais Street this afternoon? We're hoping to find a new apartment...OK, good. See you soon.
A L'APPARTEMENT	AT THE APARTMENT
Margot: C'est magnifique! Il y a _____ une _____, une _____ ...tout!	This is great! There are three large bedrooms, a terrace, a pretty living room ...everything!
Annick: _____ de payer le loyer maintenant?	Do we need to pay the rent now?
Patrick: Non, pas maintenant...Mon dieu! Les femmes _____ vite _____ appartements!	No, not now...My Gosh! Women choose their apartments fast!
Annick: _____ de trouver un logement comme ça.	We're lucky to find a place like this.
Margot: Moi, j'aime surtout le lave-vaisselle dans la cuisine. _____!	I especially like the dishwasher in the kitchen. I hate to do the dishes!

FRENCH 101
SPRING, 1982
FINAL EXAM

NOM: ______________________________

I. Reading comprehension. Read the following passage and then answer the questions on its content. (10 points)

Monsieur Dumontier est propriétaire d'un magasin où l'on vend des instruments de musique. Ses journées sont pénibles (painful) parce qu'il trouve insupportable (too much to bear) cette musique moderne qu'il doit écouter. Le soir quand il rentre à la maison, il désire le silence. Mais c'est impossible: sa fille téléphone à ses amis; son fils joue du tambour, des cymbales et de la guitare électrique. Madame Dumontier joue du piano; le chien (dog) aboie pour accompagner les musiciens.

Enfin, Dieu merci, c'est l'heure d'aller au lit. Monsieur Dumontier, épuisé, s'endort (falls asleep) immédiatement. A deux heures du matin, sa femme le réveille.

--François, lève-toi (get up)! Il y a des voleurs (thieves) dans la maison!

--Ah non, Thérèse. Comment le sais-tu (know)? demande-t-il.

--Ne perds pas de temps à me poser des questions! Je te dis (tell) qu'il y a des voleurs dans la maison. Ils peuvent nous tuer pendant que tu poses tes questions ridicules. Tu as peur de protéger ta famille, peut-être?

--Mais comment sais-tu qu'il y a des voleurs ici?

--Je peux les entendre, répond-elle, furieuse.

--Ne sois pas bête, Thérèse. Les voleurs ne font pas de bruit.

Quelques minutes plus tard, Mme Dumontier réveille de nouveau son mari.

--François, lève-toi! Je suis sûre qu'il y a des voleurs dans la maison.

--Je viens de te dire que les voleurs ne font pas de bruit.

--C'est pourquoi je suis sûre maintenant qu'ils sont dans la maison: je n'entends rien!

A. Choose the phrase that correctly completes the sentence. (5 points)

1. Monsieur Dumontier aime bien...
    a) écouter les instruments de musique.
    b) se reposer dans un endroit tranquille.
    c) la musique moderne.
    d) les journées pénibles au magasin.

2. Il n'y a pas de silence chez M. Dumontier parce que (qu')...
    a) son fils joue du piano.
    b) sa fille aboie.
    c) il y a beaucoup de bruit.
    d) sa femme parle continuellement.

3. Pendant la nuit M. Dumontier...
   a) dort comme un bébé.
   b) est réveillé par sa femme.
   c) entend des voleurs.
   d) écoute encore de la musique.

4. Madame Dumontier a peur...
   a) des voleurs.
   b) de son mari.
   c) des questions bêtes.
   d) de sa famille.

5. A la fin de l'histoire, elle pense qu'il y a des voleurs parce que (qu')...
   a) ils vont la tuer.
   b) son mari a peur.
   c) ils font du bruit.
   d) ils ne font pas de bruit.[38]

B. Go back to the words that are underlined in the story and, judging from the context, choose the best English equivalent for each one from the choices below. (5 points)

1. propriétaire
   a) janitor
   b) owner
   c) customer
   d) realtor

2. aboie
   a) yawns
   b) barks
   c) plays dead
   d) falls asleep

3. épuisé
   a) happy
   b) quiet
   c) exhausted
   d) angry

4. réveille
   a) wakes up
   b) reveals
   c) talks with
   d) hits

5. tuer
   a) call
   b) find
   c) protect
   d) kill

II. Une boulangerie à Rouen. M. et Mme Duval ont une belle petite boulangerie à Rouen. Mme Duval parle de leur vie. Complétez le passage avec des articles. (10 points)

Si vous venez à notre boulangerie, vous pouvez acheter _____ pain, _____ gâteux, _____ tartes, _____ éclairs, et beaucoup _____ bonnes choses. Nous n'avons pas _____ employé, alors nous faisons _____ pâtisseries nous-mêmes (ourselves). On n'a pas assez _____ argent maintenant, mais on a _____ optimisme et _____ courage.

Nous quittons notre lit à 4 heures du matin, pour commencer _____ travail. Il est nécessaire de faire _____ croissants et _____ baguettes pour _____ premiers clients. Si on a faim, on prend _____ croissant avec _____ beurre et un peu _____ café.

Bien sûr, nous avons nos pâtisseries préférées. Mon mari adore _____ éclairs au chocolat, mais moi, j'aime mieux _____ tarte aux fraises. Nous avons _____ chance d'avoir une boulangerie, n'est-ce pas?

un	le	de
une	la	d'
	les	du
		de la
		de l'
		des

III. Complétez le passage suivant avec les verbes encadrés. Utilisez chaque verbe <u>une</u> fois seulement. (17 points)

<u>Le week-end</u>

Quand la semaine ______, le week-end commence, n'est-ce pas? Georges, un étudiant typique, a toujours quelque chose d'intéressant à faire. Le vendredi, après son dernier cours, il ______ à son appartement et à cinq heures et demie, il ______ le dîner...mais au restaurant, bien sûr! Les étudiants comme Georges ne ______ jamais le week-end parce qu'ils ______ d'habitude, avec leurs amis.

dormir
finir
prendre
rentrer
sortir

Qu'est-ce que vous ______ le week-end? Quand nous ______ rester à l'appartement pour étudier nous ______ une grande partie du week-end!! Puisque (since) vous ______ de passer beaucoup d'examens, maintenant il est nécessaire de vous amuser!

venir
faire
perdre
devoir

Quand vos parents vous _____ le samedi soir et personne ne _____ au téléphone, est-ce qu'ils _____ inquiets (worried)? Dites-leur qu'ils _____ vous écrire des lettres et que vous allez répondre bientôt!

pouvoir
appeler
devenir
répondre

J'aime beaucoup le week-end. Je _____ toujours à lire un bon roman. Et toi, _____-tu sortir avec tes copains? Ne _____ pas! Je ne vais pas le _____ à tes parents!

dire
vouloir
mentir
tenir

IV. <u>Incomplete translation</u>. Fill in the blanks with the French equivalents of the English translation. (19 points; 1 point each, except where indicated)

P.: Salut, Marie. Ça va? P.: Hi, Mary. How are you?

M.:	Salut, Pierre. Oui, ça va, merci.	M.:	Hi, Pierre. I'm fine, thanks.
P.:	Georges et toi, qu'est-ce que vous faites ce week-end?	P.:	You and George, what are you doing this weekend?
M.:	Demain, je ___ et Georges va à Chicago pour acheter ___. (2)	M.:	Tomorrow I'm doing the housework and George is going to Chicago to buy a pretty new red car.
P.:	Vous ____ ____? (2)	P.:	You don't have your big American car any more?
M.:	Non, elle est trop ____.	M.:	No, it's too old.
P.:	Félicitations. ____ au cinéma pour fêter ça.	P.:	Congratulations. Let's go to the movies to celebrate.
M.:	Ah, merci, mais ce n'est pas possible. Ce soir nous avons des invités chez nous. _____ amis, Natalie et Marc, viennent et ils amènent _____ enfants. Et il y a aussi ____ cousine Bette et ____ ami Louis et ____ petite amie. Est-ce que tu ____ venir? ____ vers 7 heures. Mais je te préviens, Georges et moi, nous _____ _____ et les invités _____.	M.:	Oh, thanks, but that's not possible. This evening we're having a party at our house. Our friends, Natalie and Mark, are coming and they're bringing their children. And then there's my cousin Betty and your friend Louis and his girl friend. Do you feel like coming? (<u>avoir</u> expression) Get there around 7 o'clock. But I'm warning you, George and I do the cooking and the guests do the dishes.
P.:	Bon, d'accord. _____ _____. Je peux apporter quelque chose?	P.:	Oh, okay. I'm already hungry. Can I bring something?
M.:	Ah, oui. Nous ____ ____ à boire. On ____ de vin quand on a des invités.	M.:	Oh yes. We have nothing to drink. You always need wine when you have guests.

V. <u>Un mois d'été de Jean-Michel</u>. Décrivez les activités pour le mois de juin de Jean-Michel. Dites (1) la date (mentionnez le jour de la semaine et écrivez la date); (2) l'heure (use unofficial time, i.e., 2 p.m. and not 14 hours); (3) l'activité. Suivez le modèle en anglais, mais vous devez écrire en français, bien sûr! (10 points)

JUIN

	1 Dîner avec Marc 17h00	2	3	4	5 Cinéma 19h45	6
7	8	9	10 Travailler à McDonalds 13h15	11	12	13
14 Jouer au tennis avec Albert 9h30	15	16	17	18	19	20
21	22	23	24	25 Partir par le train pour Chicago 12h10	26	27

MODÈLE: (To be given in French) Thursday, June tenth at one-fifteen p.m., Jean-Michel is going to work at McDonald's. (Give this information in French for answer to 1, below.)

1. ______________________________

2. ______________________________

3. ______________________________

4. ______________________________

5. ______________________________

VI. Questions personnelles. Choisissez huit (8) questions et répondez à ces questions avec deux ou trois phrases complètes. (24 points)

A. Où habitez-vous à l'université? Décrivez votre chambre universitaire.

B. Qu'est-ce que vous étudiez à l'université? Combien de cours avez-vous? Quels sont les jours où vous allez à ces cours et à quelle heure allez-vous en cours?

C. Comment trouvez-vous la vie universitaire?

D. Quel est votre repas préféré et qu'est-ce que vous mangez et buvez à ce repas?

E. Qu'est-ce que vous faites quand vous êtes libre (free)? Où allez-vous quand vous sortez, avec qui, et quand revenez-vous?

F. Qu'est-ce qu'on doit faire pour réussir à l'université?

G. A votre avis, qu'est-ce qu'un professeur doit faire pour être un bon professeur?

H. Décrivez une semaine typique devant la télévision. A quelle heure allumez-vous (turn on) la télévision? Quelle sont vos émissions préférées?

I. Si vous ne regardez jamais la télévision, dites pourquoi.

J. A qui écrivez-vous des lettres? Combien de lettres écrivez-vous par semaine? Qu'est-ce que vous dites dans vos lettres? Si vous n'écrivez pas, dites pourquoi et ce que vous faites.

K. Qu'est-ce que vous lisez pour le plaisir (fun) ou pour apprendre les nouvelles du jour? Où lisez-vous et quand?

VII. Une lettre. Lisez le passage suivant. Il y a beaucoup de noms répétés. Ces noms sont soulignés (underlined). Remplacez les noms soulignés par des pronoms, et écrivez le passage une seconde fois (time). (7 points)

Monique écrit une lettre à sa famille. Elle écrit la lettre dans sa chambre à la cité universitaire. Sa chambre est très jolie et tranquille. Elle trouve sa chambre très sympathique.

Dans sa chambre, il y a beaucoup de jolies affiches. Elle adore ces affiches parce qu'elles rendent la chambre intime. Elle a une affiche avec une photo de John Travolta. Elle regarde John Travolta chaque soir avant de se coucher (to go to bed). Elle adore le film "Urban Cowboy." Elle va voir ce film avec des amis mardi soir.

Dans sa lettre, Monique ne parle pas de ses cours. Elle ne discute pas ses cours parce qu'elle a trop de travail. C'est la fin du semestre, et elle veut oublier (forget) ses cours.

Maintenant, écrivez le paragraphe encore une fois, et utilisez des pronoms au lieu des noms soulignés.

Monique écrit une lettre à sa famille. ____________________.
Sa chambre est très jolie et tranquille. ____________________.
Dans sa chambre, il y a beaucoup de jolies affiches.
____________________. Elle a une affiche avec une photo de John Travolta. ____________________. Elle adore le film "Urban Cowboy." ____________________.
Dans sa lettre, Monique ne parle pas de ses cours.
____________________. C'est la fin du semestre, ____________________.

VIII. Composition. Choisissez un (1) sujet de composition seulement. Ecrivez un minimum de douze (12) phrases. (10 points)

A. Ecrivez une lettre à un(e) ami(e). Dans votre lettre vous pouvez parler de cette semaine et de ce que vous venez de faire, de vos impressions de la vie universitaire, et de vos projets pour les vacances d'été.

Expressions utiles à employer: venir de, aimer, détester, préférer, espérer, essayer, réussir à, apprendre, passer un examen, aller + inf.

B. Décrivez votre famille et la maison où elle habite. Vous pouvez décrire les membres de votre famille et ce qu'ils font à la maison. Décrivez la maison: combien de pièces y a-t-il, quelles sont ces pièces, quelles sont vos pièces préférées et pourquoi?

Expressions utiles: les expressions avec faire, manger, lire, regarder, écouter, jouer à, jouer de, dormir.

IX. Compréhension culturelle. Read the following dialogues in which there has been a misunderstanding due to some cultural factors that the people involved do not understand. Then choose the best explanation of the misunderstanding, using your own knowledge of the French way of life. (3 points)

SITUATION A. Deux Américains étudient à la bibliothèque à Paris.

John: Bonjour les Françaises. Je m'appelle John Ward et voici mon camarade Paul Brett. Comment vous appelez-vous?

Marie-Eve: Bonjour. Voici Fabienne Britton, et moi, je m'appelle Marie-Eve Boulard.

Paul: Enchanté, Fabienne et Marie-Eve. Fabienne veux-tu me passer ce livre-là s'il te plaît....Merci. Es-tu étudiante à la Sorbonne?

Fabienne: Non....Marie-Eve, on y va?

(Les deux jeunes filles partent.)

John: What happened? They sure didn't want to talk to us!

Paul: No....They weren't very friendly...perhaps French girls are just like that.

Why did the girls leave?

1) French girls don't like American men.
2) The Americans were too informal with them.
3) They had to rush off to class.
4) They were finished studying.

SITUATION B. Au restaurant universitaire, un Américain prend le petit déjeuner avec un Français.

Greg: Bonjour Pierre, as-tu faim?

Pierre: Ah oui! Je vais prendre un croissant, un pain au chocolat, et du café. Qu'est-ce que tu prends?

Greg: Je vais commander deux oeufs au plat, du jambon, du jus d'orange et du café.

(Le serveur apporte le menu. Ils le regardent.)

Greg: Quoi! Je ne comprends pas! Où sont les oeufs, le jambon, et le jus d'orange? Quel restaurant!

(Pierre rigole.)

Why didn't Greg find what he wanted on the menu?
1) It was a cheap restaurant.
2) He couldn't read French very well.
3) The typical French breakfast is light.

SITUATION C. Kathy et Julie cherchent la propriétaire d'un appartement mais elles ne peuvent pas la trouver. Elles vont au kiosque au coin de la rue.

Julie: Pardon Monsieur. Est-ce que vous savez où habite Madame Debroie?

Monsieur: Pourquoi est-ce que vous la cherchez?

Kathy: Nous voulons louer un de ses appartements.

Monsieur: D'accord....Elle habite au troisième étage, dans le grand bâtiment là-bas.

Julie: Merci.

(Elles partent mais elles ne la trouvent pas. Elles retournent au kiosque.)

Kathy: Monsieur, elle n'habite pas au troisième étage!

Monsieur: Écoutez! C'est une de mes meilleures amies et je sais où elle habite!!

Why couldn't the girls find the woman?
1) The man wanted to trick them.
2) They went to the wrong building.
3) The girls didn't understand French very well.
4) The third floor in France is the 4th floor in the U.S.[39]

APPENDIX B

Oral Proficiency Rating Scales

ORAL PROFICIENCY RATING SCALES[40]

ACADEMIC (ACTFL/ETS) RATING SCALE			GOVERNMENT (ILR) RATING SCALE
NO ABILITY WHATSOEVER IN THE LANGUAGE	0	LEVEL 0	NO FUNCTIONAL ABILITY IN THE LANGUAGE
Unable to function in the spoken language. Oral production is limited to occasional isolated words. Essentially no communicative ability.	NOVICE LOW		
Able to operate only in a very limited capacity within very predictable areas of need. Vocabulary limited to that necessary to express simple elementary needs and basic courtesy formulae. Syntax is fragmented, inflections and word endings frequently omitted, confused or distorted and the majority of utterances consist of isolated words or short formulae. Utterances do not show evidence of creating with language or being able to cope with the simplest situations. They are marked by repetition of an interlocutor's words as well as by frequent long pauses. Pronunciation is frequently unintelligible and is strongly influenced by first language. Can be understood only with difficulty, even by persons such as teachers who are used to speaking with non-native speakers.	NOVICE MID		
Able to satisfy immediate needs using learned utterances. There is no real autonomy of expression, although there are some emerging signs of spontaneity and flexibility. There is a slight increase in utterance length but frequent long pauses and repetition of interlocutor's words may still occur. Can ask questions or make statements with reasonable accuracy only where this involves short memorized utterances or formulae. Most utterances are telegraphic and word endings are often omitted, confused or distorted. Vocabulary is limited to areas of immediate survival needs. Can produce most phonemes but when they are combined in words or groups of words, errors are frequent and, in spite of repetition, may severely inhibit communication even with persons used to dealing with such learners. Little development in stress and intonation is evident.	NOVICE HIGH	LEVEL* 0+	Able to satisfy immediate needs using learned utterances. There is no real autonomy of expression, although there may be some emerging signs of spontaneity and flexibility. There is a slight increase in utterance length but frequent long pauses and repetition of interlocutor's words still occur. Can ask questions or make statements with reasonable accuracy only where this involves short memorized utterances or formulae. Most utterances are telegraphic and word endings (both inflectional and non-inflectional) are often omitted, confused or distorted. Vocabulary is limited to areas of immediate survival needs. Can differentiate most phonemes when produced in isolation but when they are combined in words or groups of words, errors are frequent and, even with repetition, may severely inhibit communication even with persons used to dealing with such learners. Little development in stress and intonation is evident. *There are only minor differences between the two descriptions at this level.

ACADEMIC (ACTFL/ETS) RATING SCALE			GOVERNMENT (ILR) RATING SCALE
Able to satisfy basic survival needs and minimum courtesy requirements. In areas of immediate need or on very familiar topics, can ask and answer simple questions, initiate and respond to simple statements, and maintain very simple face-to-face conversations. When asked to do so, is able to formulate some questions with limited constructions and much inaccuracy. Almost every utterance contains fractured syntax and other grammatical errors. Vocabulary inadequate to express anything but the most elementary needs. Strong interference from L_1 occurs in articulation, stress and intonation. Misunderstandings frequently arise from limited vocabulary and grammar and erroneous phonology but, with repetition, can generally be understood by native speakers in regular contact with foreigners attempting to speak their language. Little precision in information conveyed owing to tentative state of grammatical development and little or no use of modifiers.	INTERMEDIATE LOW	LEVEL 1	Able to satisfy routine travel needs and minimum courtesy requirements. Can ask and answer questions on very familiar topics; within the scope of the very limited language experience can understand simple questions and statements, allowing for slowed speech, repetition or paraphrase; speaking vocabulary inadequate to express anything but the most elementary needs; errors in pronunciation and grammar are frequent, but can be understood by a native speaker used to dealing with foreigners attempting to speak the language; while topics which are "very familiar" and elementary needs vary considerably from individual to individual, any person at the S-1 level should be able to order a simple meal, ask for shelter or lodging, ask and give simple directions, make purchases and tell time.
Able to satisfy some survival needs and some limited social demands. Some evidence of grammatical accuracy in basic constructions, e.g., subject-verb agreement, noun-adjective agreement, some notion of inflection. Vocabulary permits discussion of topics beyond basic survival needs, e.g., personal history, leisure time activities. Is able to formulate some questions when asked to do so.	INTERMEDIATE MID		
Able to satisfy most survival needs and limited social demands. Developing flexibility in a range of circumstances beyond immediate survival needs. Shows spontaneity in language production but fluency is very uneven. Can initiate and sustain a general conversation but has little understanding of the social conventions of conversation. Limited vocabulary range necessitates much hesitation and circumlocution. The commoner tense forms occur but errors are frequent in formation and selection. Can use most question forms. While some word order is established, errors still occur in more complex patterns. Cannot sustain coherent structures in longer utterances or unfamiliar situations. Ability to describe and give precise information is limited. Aware of basic cohesive features (e.g., pronouns, verb inflections), but many are unreliable, especially if less immediate in reference. Extended discourse is largely a series of short, discrete utterances. Articulation is comprehensible to native speakers used to dealing with foreigners, and can combine most phonemes with reasonable comprehensibility, but still has difficulty in producing certain sounds, in certain positions, or in certain combinations, and speech will usually be labored. Still has to repeat utterances frequently to be understood by the general public. Able to produce narration in either past or future.	INTERMEDIATE HIGH	LEVEL 1+	Able to satisfy most survival needs and limited social demands. Developing flexibility in a range of circumstances beyond immediate survival needs. Shows some spontaneity in language production but fluency is very uneven. Can initiate and sustain a general conversation but has little understanding of the social conventions of conversation. Limited vocabulary range necessitates much hesitation and circumlocution. The commoner tense forms occur but errors are frequent in formation and selection. Can use most question forms. While some word order is established, errors still occur in more complex patterns. Cannot sustain coherent structures in longer utterances or unfamiliar situations. Ability to describe and give precise information is limited. Aware of basic cohesive features (e.g., pronouns, verb inflections), but many are unreliable, especially if less immediate in reference. Extended discourse is largely a series of short discrete utterances. Articulation is comprehensible to native speakers used to dealing with foreigners, and can combine most phonemes with reasonable comprehensibility, but still has difficulty in producing certain sounds, in certain positions, or in certain combinations, and speech will usually be labored. Still has to repeat utterances frequently to be understood by the general public. Able to produce some narration in either past or future.

ACADEMIC (ACTFL/ETS) RATING SCALE			GOVERNMENT (ILR) RATING SCALE
Able to satisfy routine social demands and limited work requirements. Can handle with confidence but not with facility most social situations including introductions and casual conversations about current events, as well as work, family, and autobiographical information; can handle limited work requirements, needing help in handling any complications or difficulties. Has a speaking vocabulary sufficient to respond simply with some circumlocutions; accent, though often quite faulty, is intelligible; can usually handle elementary constructions quite accurately but does not have thorough or confident control of the grammar.	ADVANCED	LEVEL 2	Able to satisfy routine social demands and limited work requirements. Can handle with confidence but not with facility most social situations including introductions and casual conversations about current events, as well as work, family, and autobiographical information; can handle limited work requirements, needing help in handling any complications or difficulties. Has a speaking vocabulary sufficient to respond simply with some circumlocutions; accent, though often quite faulty is intelligible; can usually handle elementary constructions quite accurately but does not have thorough or confident control of the grammar.
Able to satisfy most work requirements and show some ability to communicate on concrete topics relating to particular interests and special fields of competence. Often shows remarkable fluency and ease of speech, but under tension or pressure language may break down. Weaknesses or unevenness in one of the foregoing or in pronunciation result in occasional miscommunication. Areas of weakness range from simple constructions such as plurals, articles, prepositions, and negatives to more complex structures such as tense usage, passive constructions, word order, and relative clauses. Normally controls general vocabulary with some groping for everyday vocabulary still evident.	ADVANCED PLUS	LEVEL 2+	Able to satisfy most work requirements and show some ability to communicate on concrete topics relating to particular interests and special fields of competence. Often shows remarkable fluency and ease of speech, but under tension or pressure language may break down. Generally strong in either grammar or vocabulary, but not in both. Weaknesses or unevenness in one of the foregoing or in pronunciation result in occasional miscommunication. Areas of weakness range from simple constructions such as tense usage, passive constructions, word order, and relative clauses. Normally controls general vocabulary with some groping for everyday vocabulary still evident. Shows some evidence of target language sociolinguistics and culture.
ALL PERFORMANCE ABOVE ADVANCED PLUS IS RATED AS SUPERIOR.	SUPERIOR	LEVEL 3	Able to speak the language with sufficient structural accuracy and vocabulary to participate effectively in most formal and informal conversations on practical, social and professional topics. Can discuss particular interests and special fields of competence with reasonable ease; comprehension is quite complete for a normal rate of speech; vocabulary is broad enough that rarely has to grope for a word; accent may be obviously foreign; control of grammar good; errors never interfere with understanding and rarely disturb the native speaker.
		LEVEL 4 REPRESENTATIONAL PROFICIENCY	Able to use the language fluently and accurately on all levels normally pertinent to professional needs. Can understand and participate in any conversation within the range of own personal and professional experience with a high degree of fluency and precision of vocabulary; would rarely be taken for a native speaker, but can respond appropriately even in unfamiliar situations; errors of pronunciation and grammar quite rare; can handle informal interpreting from and into the language.
		LEVEL 5 NATIVE OR BILINGUAL PROFICIENCY	Speaking proficiency equivalent to that of an educated native speaker. Has complete fluency in the language such that speech on all levels is fully accepted by educated native speakers in all of its features, including breadth of vocabulary and idiom, colloquialisms, and pertinent cultural references.

NOTES

1. A design for measuring and communicating foreign language proficiency. ACTFL, U.S. Department of Education Grant #G00 8103203. For more information, write to David Hiple, Project Director, ACTFL, 579 Broadway, Hastings-on-Hudson, NY 10706.

2. For a discussion of the perceived need among language teachers for a common standard of measurement, see Regina H. Paul, Needed: Stepladders of foreign language learning, *Foreign Language Annals* 14 (December 1981), pp. 379-84.

3. The proficiency definitions referred to here correspond to the 0-5 ratings of the ILR scale, which was derived from the FSI definitions and updated in 1982 by government schools participating in the Interagency Language Roundtable. These definitions are part of the ACTFL/ETS Stepladder Project described earlier. See footnote (1) and Appendix B.

4. The term "absolute" proficiency implies that the range of language skills being tested is not limited to specific curricula, courses of study, or amount of time spent in learning the language, but rather represents the candidate's "general" proficiency in the language at a given point in time, as compared with the "educated native speaker" as an absolute standard.

5. William R. Slager, Creating contexts for language practice, in *Developing communication skills* (Rowley, MA: Newbury House, 1978), pp. 74-75.

6. Adapted from Rebecca M. Valette, *Modern language testing*, 2nd ed. (New York: Harcourt Brace Jovanovich, 1977).

7. Example provided by Elaine Sunnen, teaching assistant, University of Illinois at Urbana-Champaign.

8. Sketch and text adapted from George Winkler et al., *Unsere Freunde* (New York: Harcourt Brace Jovanovich, 1978), p. 199, by Sylvaine Mella, teaching assistant, University of Illinois at Urbana-Champaign.

9. Patricia Boylan.

10. Adapted from Gilbert A. Jarvis et al., *Connâitre et se connâitre* (New York: Holt, Rinehart and Winston, 1976).

11. Jean-Noël Rey and G. V. Santoni, *Quand les français parlent* (Rowley, MA: Newbury House, 1975), p. 37. Reprinted by permission.

12. Patricia Boylan.

13. *Ontario Assessment Instrument Pool/French as a second language: Junior and intermediate divisions (grades 6 and 10)* (Toronto: Ministry of Education, Ontario, 1980), Item No. 13019. Reprinted by permission.

14. Ibid., Item No. 11014.02. Reprinted by permission.

15. Françoise Howard, Testing communicative performance in French as a second language, *Canadian Modern Language Review* 36 (January 1980), p. 277.

16. *Ontario Assessment Instrument Pool*, Item No. 33031. Reprinted by permission.

17. This does not necessarily *have* to be the case, however. One can test cohesive elements of discourse, such as pronouns, adverbial connectors, etc. in such a way that decisions require crossing sentence boundaries.

18. Example provided by Jeri Guthrie, teaching assistant, University of Illinois at Urbana-Champaign.

19. John Oller, Discrete-point tests vs. tests of integrative skills, in *Focus on the learner: Pragmatic perspectives for the language teacher* (Rowley, MA: Newbury House, 1973), p. 191.

20. Adapted from Judith Muyskens, Alice Omaggio et al., *Rendez-vous* (New York: Random House, 1982), pp. 428-29.

21. Paragraph taken from Lucien F. Baker et al., *Collage: Variétés culturelles* (New York: Random House, 1981), p. 67. Reprinted by permission.

22. *Ontario Assessment Instrument Pool*, Item No. 31068. Reprinted by permission.

23. Ibid., Item No. 32000.03. Reprinted by permission.

24. Josephine D'Alleva and Annamaria Bee, Incontri culturali (Skokie, IL: National Textbook Co., 1977), p. 32. Reprinted by permission.

25. Adapted from Boylan.

26. Judith Muyskens, Alice Omaggio et al., Rendez-vous, p. 301.

27. Adapted from Boylan.

28. Sketch and text adapted from George Winkler et al., Unsere Freunde (New York: Harcourt Brace Jovanovich, 1978), p. 197, by Sylvaine Mella, teaching assistant, University of Illinois at Urbana-Champaign. Sketch revised by Sonia Kundert, Center for Applied Linguistics.

29. Adapted from Muyskens, Omaggio et al., Rendez-vous, Workbook, p. 131.

30. Muyskens, Omaggio et al., p. 284.

31. Adapted from Muyskens, Omaggio et al., p. 91.

32. Françoise Howard, Testing communicative performance, p. 279.

33. Muyskens, Omaggio et al., p. 354.

34. For sample items, see Albert Valdman, Testing communicative ability at the university level, ADFL Bulletin 13 (November 1981).

35. Adapted from Thérèse Bonin and Diane Birckbichler, Real communication through conversation and interview cards, Modern Language Journal 59 (January/February 1975), pp. 22-25.

36. See Kramsch (1981) for an extensive list of these and other discourse expressions in French and German.

37. Test created by Sue Siltman, graduate teaching assistant, Department of Spanish, Italian, and Portuguese, University of Illinois at Urbana-Champaign.

38. Story reprinted and questions in Part A adapted from June K. Phillips, Petites contes sympathiques (Skokie, IL: National Textbook Co., 1979), pp. 38-40. Reprinted by permission.

39. Adapted from Arley W. Levno, Rencontres culturelles (Skokie, IL: National Textbook Co., 1977).

40. From Judith Liskin-Gasparro, ETS oral proficiency testing manual (Princeton, NJ: Educational Testing Service, 1982).

REFERENCES

Most documents identified by an ED number may be read on microfiche at an ERIC library collection or ordered from the ERIC Document Reproduction Service, P.O. Box 190, Arlington, VA 22210.

Baker, Lucien et al. 1981. Collage: Variétés culturelles. New York: Random House.

Bartz, Walter H. 1976. Testing communicative competence. In R. Schulz, ed., Teaching for communication in the foreign language classroom. (Papers of the 1976 Central States Conference on the Teaching of Foreign Languages.) Skokie, IL: National Textbook Co. ED 134 023.

_____. 1979. Testing oral communication in the foreign language classroom. Language in Education series, No. 17. Arlington, VA: Center for Applied Linguistics/ERIC Clearinghouse on Languages and Linguistics. ED 176 590.

Bondaruk, John, J. Child and E. Tetrault. 1975. Contextual testing. In R. Jones and B. Spolsky, eds., Testing language proficiency. Arlington, VA: Center for Applied Linguistics. ED 107 161.

Boylan, Patricia C. Personal communication.

Canale, Michael and Merrill Swain. 1980. Communicative approaches to second language teaching and testing. Applied Linguistics 1 (Spring): 1-47.

D'Alleva, Josephine and Annamaria Bee. 1977. Incontri culturali. Skokie, IL: National Textbook Co.

Gaies, Stephen J. 1980. Language testing and the notion of 'authenticity.' Paper presented at the Kentucky Foreign Language Conference. ED 202 239.

Higgs, Theodore and Ray Clifford. 1982. The push towards communication. In T. Higgs, ed., Curriculum, competence and the foreign language teacher. The ACTFL Foreign Language Education Series, vol. 13. Skokie, IL: National Textbook Co. ED 210 908.

Hosenfeld, Carol. 1976. Learning about learning: Discovering our students' strategies. Foreign Language Annals 9 (April): 117-29.

Howard, Françoise. 1980. Testing communicative performance in French as a second language: A search for procedures. Canadian Modern Language Review 36 (January): 272-89.

Jarvis, Gilbert et al. 1976. Connaître et se connaître. New York: Holt, Rinehart and Winston.

Jones, Randall and Bernard Spolsky. 1975. Testing language proficiency. Arlington, VA: Center for Applied Linguistics. ED 107 161.

Kramsch, Claire. 1981. Discourse analysis and second language teaching. Language in Education series, No. 37. Washington, DC: Center for Applied Linguistics/ERIC Clearinghouse on Languages and Linguistics. ED 208 675.

Levno, Arley W. Rencontres culturelles. 1977. Skokie, IL: National Textbook Co.

Linder, Cathy. 1977. Oral communication testing: A handbook for the foreign language teacher. Skokie, IL: National Textbook Co.

Liskin-Gasparro, Judith. 1982. ETS oral proficiency testing manual. Princeton, NJ: Educational Testing Service.

Mauriac, Paul. 1980. La compréhension du français parlé au niveau avancé: un exemple de test. Français dans le Monde 152 (April): 34-40.

Muyskens, Judith, Alice Omaggio et al. 1982. Rendez-vous. New York: Random House.

Oller, John W. 1973. Discrete-point tests vs. tests of integrative skills. In J. Oller and J. Richards, eds., Focus on the learner: Pragmatic perspectives for the language teacher. Rowley, MA: Newbury House.

_____. 1975. Dictation: A test of grammar-based expectancies. In R. Jones and B. Spolsky, eds., Testing language proficiency. Arlington, VA: Center for Applied Linguistics. ED 107 161.

_____ and J. C. Richards, eds. 1973. Focus on the learner: Pragmatic perspectives for the language teacher. Rowley, MA: Newbury House.

Omaggio, Alice C. 1981. Priorities in classroom testing for the 1980s. In Proceedings of the National Conference on Professional Priorities. Hastings-on-Hudson, NY: ACTFL Materials Center. ED 212 166.

_____. 1981. Helping learners succeed: Activities for the foreign language classroom. Language in Education series, No. 36. Washington, DC: Center for Applied Linguistics/ERIC Clearinghouse on Languages and Linguistics. ED 208 674.

_____. 1982. Games and interaction activities for the development of functional proficiency in a second language. Canadian Modern Language Review 38 (Spring): 517-46.

_____. In press. The proficiency-oriented classroom. In T. Higgs, ed. Proficiency: The organizing principle. The ACTFL Foreign Language Education Series, vol. 15. Skokie, IL: National Textbook Co.

Ontario Assessment Instrument Pool/French as a second language: Junior and intermediate divisions (grades 6 and 10). 1980. Toronto: Ministry of Education, Ontario.

Paul, Regina H. 1981. Needed: Stepladders of foreign language learning. Foreign Language Annals 14 (December): 379-84.

Popyuk, William. 1980. A model for an item bank in second language proficiency testing. System 8 (January): 47-52.

Proceedings of the national conference on professional priorities. 1981. Hastings-on-Hudson, NY: ACTFL Materials Center. ED 212 166.
Schulz, Renate A. and Walter Bartz. 1975. Free to communicate. In G. Jarvis, ed. Perspective: A new freedom. The ACTFL Foreign Language Education Series, vol. 7. Skokie, IL: National Textbook Co. ED 159 880.
Shohamy, Elana. 1982. Affective considerations in language teaching. Modern Language Journal 66 (Spring): 13-17.
Slager, William R. 1978. Creating contexts for language practice. In E. Joiner and P. Westphal, eds., Developing communication skills. Rowley, MA: Newbury House.
Snyder, Barbara. 1977. Encuentras culturales. Skokie, IL: National Textbook Co.
Valdman, Albert. 1981. Testing communicative ability at the university level. ADFL Bulletin 13 (November): 1-5.
Valette, Rebecca M. 1977. Modern language testing. 2nd ed. New York: Harcourt Brace Jovanovich.
_____. 1978. Developing and evaluating communication skills in the classroom. In E. Joiner and P. Westphal, eds., Developing communication skills. Rowley, MA: Newbury House.
Wesche, M. 1981. Communicative testing in a second language. Canadian Modern Language Review 37 (March): 551-71.
Winkler, George et al. 1978. Unsere Freunde. New York: Harcourt Brace Jovanovich.
Woodford, Protase E. 1980. Foreign language testing. Modern Language Journal 64 (Spring): 97-102.

Additional Reading

Brown, James D. 1980. Relative merits of four methods of scoring cloze tests. Modern Language Journal 64 (Autumn): 311-17.
Jorstad, Helen L. 1980. New approaches to assessment of language learning. In T. Geno, ed., Our profession: Present status and future directions 1980. Reports of the Northeast Conference on the Teaching of Foreign Languages. Middlebury, VT: Northeast Conference.
Lange, Dale and Ray Clifford. 1980. Testing in foreign languages, ESL, and bilingual education, 1966-1979: A select, annotated ERIC bibliography. Language in Education series, No. 24. Arlington, VA: Center for Applied Linguistics/ERIC Clearinghouse on Languages and Linguistics. ED 183 027.
Shirer, Robert K. Kulturelle Begegnungen. 1977. Skokie, IL: National Textbook Co.
Silverstein, Raymond, ed. 1979. Proceedings of the third international conference on frontiers in language proficiency and dominance testing. Carbondale, IL: Southern Illinois University. ED 144 394 - 144 412.

Alice C. Omaggio (Ph.D., The Ohio State University) is assistant professor in the Department of French at the University of Illinois at Urbana-Champaign, where she coordinates beginning and intermediate courses, supervises teaching assistants, and teaches various courses in language acquisition and methodology. She was associate director of the ERIC Clearinghouse on Languages and Linguistics from 1977-79, and is currently a member of the ACTFL Executive Council. Her publications have appeared in various professional journals and compilations, including *Foreign Language Annals*, the *Modern Language Journal*, the *ACTFL Review*, the *Central States Conference Reports*, the *Northeast Conference Reports*, and the *Language in Education* series of the Center for Applied Linguistics. Dr. Omaggio coedited the 1976 *Central States Conference Reports* and is the coauthor of three college-level textbooks for beginning and intermediate French published by Random House.

LANGUAGE IN EDUCATION: THEORY AND PRACTICE

The Language in Education series can be purchased by volume or by individual titles. The subscription rate is $37.00 for Volume 1; $43.00 for Volume 2; $49.00 for Volume 3; $56.50 for Volume 4; and $45.50 for Volume 5. Add $1.50 postage and handling charges for individual orders. ALL ORDERS MUST BE PREPAID. To subscribe to the complete series of publications, write to:

Center for Applied Linguistics
Box 4866, Hampden Station
Baltimore MD 21211

Below is a selected list of series titles:

Volume 1 (1977-78)

6. From the Community to the Classroom: Gathering Second-Language Speech Samples, by Barbara F. Freed. $2.95. ED 157 404
7. Kinesics and Cross-Cultural Understanding, by Genelle G. Morain. $2.95. ED 157 405
8. New Perspectives on Teaching Vocabulary, by Howard H. Keller. $2.95. ED 157 406
9. Teacher Talk: Language in the Classroom, by Shirley B. Heath. $2.95. ED 158 575
10. Language and Linguistics: Bases for a Curriculum, by Julia S. Falk. $2.95. ED 158 576
11. Teaching Culture: Strategies and Techniques, by Robert C. Lafayette. $2.95. ED 157 407
12. Personality and Second Language Learning, by Virginia D. Hodge. $2.95. ED 157 408

Volume 2 (1978-79)

13. Games and Simulations in the Foreign Language Classroom, by Alice C. Omaggio. $5.95. ED 177 887
16. Foreign Languages, English as a Second/Foreign Language, and the U.S. Multinational Corporation, by Marianne Inman. $6.75. ED 179 089
17. Testing Oral Communication in the Foreign Language Classroom, by Walter H. Bartz. $2.95. ED 176 590
18. Intensive Foreign Language Courses, by David P. Benseler and Renate A. Schulz. $4.95. ED 176 587
19. Evaluating a Second Language Program, by Gilbert A. Jarvis and Shirley J. Adams. $2.95. ED 176 589
20. Reading a Second Language, by G. Truett Cates and Janet K. Swaffar. $2.95. ED 176 588

Volume 3 (1979-80)

24. Testing in Foreign Languages, ESL, and Bilingual Education, 1966-1979: A Select, Annotated ERIC Bibliography, compiled by Dale L. Lange and Ray T. Clifford. $7.95. ED 183 027
25. ACTFL 1979: Abstracts of Presented Papers. $5.95. ED 183 031

26. A Guide to Language Camps in the United States, by Lois Vines. $3.95. ED 183 030
28. Teaching a Second Language: A Guide for the Student Teacher, by Constance K. Knop. $4.95. ED 195 165
29. Assessing Study Abroad Programs for Secondary School Students, by Helene Z. Loew. $2.95. ED 193 974
30. Chinese Language Study in American Higher Education: State of the Art, by Peter A. Eddy, James J. Wrenn, and Sophia A. Behrens. $7.95. ED 195 166
31. Sentence Combining in Second Language Instruction, by Thomas C. Cooper, Genelle Morain, and Theodore Kalivoda. $7.95. ED 195 167
32. Teaching the Metric System in the Foreign Language Classroom, by Bette Le Feber Stevens. $4.95. ED 195 168

Volume 4 (1980-81)

33. Directory of Foreign Language Service Organizations: 2, by Sophia A. Behrens. $7.00. ED 208 671
34. The Older Foreign Language Learner: A Challenge for Colleges and Universities, by Elizabeth G. Joiner. $4.00. ED 208 672
36. Helping Learners Succeed: Activities for the Foreign Language Classroom, by Alice C. Omaggio. $5.00. ED 208 674
37. Discourse Analysis and Second Language Teaching, by Claire J. Kramsch. $7.00. ED 208 675
39. Teaching French as a Multicultural Language: The French-Speaking World Outside of Europe, by John D. Ogden. $4.50. ED 208 677
40. PR Prototypes: A Guidebook for Promoting Foreign Language Study to the Public, by Rosanne G. Royer and Lester W. McKim. $7.00. ED 208 678

Volume 5 (1981-82)

43. Teaching Writing in the Foreign Language Curriculum, by Claire Gaudiani. $8.95 paper/$15.95 cloth. ED 209 961
44. Functional-Notional Concepts: Adapting the FL Textbook, by Gail Guntermann and June K. Phillips. $6.00. ED 217 698
47. Children's Second Language Learning, by Barry McLaughlin. $7.00. ED 217 701
48. Creative Activities for the Second Language Classroom, by Diane W. Birckbichler. $8.95. ED 217 702
50. Error Correction Techniques for the FL Classroom, by Joel C. Walz. $5.75. ED 217 704

Volume 6 (1982-83)

52. Proficiency-Oriented Classroom Testing, by Alice C. Omaggio.
53. A Guide to Language Camps in the U.S.: 2, by Lois Vines.
54. Teaching Hearing-Impaired Children in Regular Classrooms, by Peter M. Blackwell.
55. The High School Goes Abroad: International Homestay Exchange Programs, by Phyllis J. Dragonas.